Educational Gymnastics for Children

Tina J. Hall, PhD

Middle Tennessee State University

Shirley Ann Holt/Hale, PhD

Linden Elementary School, Oak Ridge, Tennessee

HUMAN KINETICS

Library of Congress Cataloging-in-Publication Data

Names: Hall, Tina J. author. | Holt/Hale, Shirley Ann author.
Title: Educational gymnastics for children / Tina J. Hall, Shirley Ann
  Holt/Hale.
Description: Champaign, IL : Human Kinetics, [2024] | Includes
  bibliographical references.
Identifiers: LCCN 2022052055 (print) | LCCN 2022052056 (ebook) | ISBN
  9781718212008 (paperback) | ISBN 9781718212015 (epub) | ISBN
  9781718212022 (pdf)
Subjects: LCSH: Gymnastics for children | Gymnastics--Study and teaching.
Classification: LCC GV464.5 .H28 2024 (print) | LCC GV464.5 (ebook) | DDC
  796.44083--dc23/ng/20221114
LC record available at https://lccn.loc.gov/2022052055
LC ebook record available at https://lccn.loc.gov/2022052056

ISBN: 978-1-7182-1200-8 (print)

The web addresses cited in this text were current as of November 2022, unless otherwise noted.

Acquisitions Editor: Scott Wikgren; **Developmental Editor:** Judy Park; **Managing Editor:** Derek Campbell; **Editorial Assistant:** Ian C. Fricker; **Copyeditor:** Bob Replinger; **Proofreader:** Leigh Keylock; **Permissions Manager:** Laurel Mitchell; **Graphic Designer:** Joe Buck; **Cover Designer:** Keri Evans; **Cover Design Specialist:** Susan Rothermel Allen; **Photograph (cover):** Photo courtesy of the authors; **Photographs (interior):** © Human Kinetics, unless otherwise noted; **Photo Asset Manager:** Laura Fitch; **Photo Production Manager:** Jason Allen; **Senior Art Manager:** Kelly Hendren; **Illustrations:** © Human Kinetics, unless otherwise noted; **Printer:** Kingery Printing – United Graphics Division

Printed in the United States of America

10 9 8 7 6 5 4 3 2 1

The paper in this book is certified under a sustainable forestry program.

Human Kinetics
1607 N. Market Street
Champaign, IL 61820
USA

United States and International
Website: **US.HumanKinetics.com**
Email: info@hkusa.com
Phone: 1-800-747-4457

Canada
Website: **Canada.HumanKinetics.com**
Email: info@hkcanada.com

E8551

To all current and future elementary physical education teachers who provide the joy of learning educational gymnastics to children. To Lee Allsbrook, Peter Werner, Cam Kerst, and my coauthor Shirley Holt/Hale for their influence in my love of teaching gymnastics.

—Tina

To the boys and girls of Linden Elementary who were the source of my joy in teaching and to my mother who was, and is, the inspiration for a lifetime of teaching and learning.

—Shirley

CONTENTS

Preface vii • Acknowledgments xi

PART I Foundation of Educational Gymnastics   1

1 Educational Gymnastics   3

Child-Centered Gymnastics 3
Laban's Movement Analysis Framework 5
Foundation of Games, Sports, and Dance 9
Summary 9

2 Balance as the Foundation for Movement   11

Balance in Gymnastics 11
Balance in Games and Sports 13
Balance in Dance 14
Balance as a Lifetime Skill 15
Summary 15

3 Establishing the Teaching and Learning Environment for Educational Gymnastics   17

Child-Centered Approach 17
Self-Responsibility and Student Success 19
Instruction Using a Child-Centered Approach 20
Safe Learning Environments 24
Summary 27

PART II Learning Experiences in Educational Gymnastics   29

4 Movement Analysis Framework   31

Teaching the Concepts and Prerequisites 31
Body Awareness 35
Space Awareness 44
Effort 49
Relationships 52
Summary 54
Appendix A 55
Appendix B 58

5   The Foundational Skills of Balance   **63**

Balance Concepts   65

Balancing Using Body Shapes and Levels   78

Summary   85

Appendix   86

6   Balance and Weight Transfer   **87**

Weight Transfer Rolling   89

Inverted Balances   96

Weight Transference Between Balances   102

Weight Transference With Levels and Shapes   109

Weight Transference Using In-Flight Actions   115

Educational Gymnastics Sequences   128

Summary   134

Appendix   135

7   Educational Gymnastics With Equipment   **137**

Establishing a Safe Environment for Gymnastics Equipment   139

Safe Balances and Travel on Equipment   143

Balances and Weight Transfer on Equipment   147

Gymnastics Equipment Mounts and Dismounts   153

Sequences on Equipment   163

Summary   169

Appendix A   170

Appendix B   173

PART III   Reflection and Assessment in Educational Gymnastics   **175**

8   Alignment of Goals, Standards, and Assessments in Educational Gymnastics   **177**

Physical Education Goals   177

National Standards   178

Assessment   180

Summary   185

Epilogue   186 • About the Authors   187

PREFACE

Welcome to the first edition of *Educational Gymnastics for Children*. The primary goal of this text is to provide teachers of elementary physical education and university students preparing to be teachers of physical education with the content and teaching strategies needed to provide students a quality program of educational gymnastics.

Educational gymnastics, based on the work of Rudolf Laban, has a rich history in the primary and junior schools of England, dating back to the early 1960s. Numerous books have been written in the United States focusing on the educational gymnastics curriculum, but most reflected the traditional gymnastics of the Olympics. *Educational Gymnastics for Children* is written by two physical education professionals who have a background in educational gymnastics and years of teaching gymnastics in the elementary physical education environment.

Educational Gymnastics for Children provides the theoretical foundation and practical application of educational gymnastics for all students. Whether you are a current teacher or a university student, this text provides you the content for presenting educational gymnastics in a child-centered approach for student learning. Highlights of the text include the following:

- The distinction between educational and traditional gymnastics
- The role of balance as the foundation of educational gymnastics
- The linkage of educational gymnastics to all sports and dance
- Balance as a lifelong life skill

The text also accomplishes the following:

- Strengthens the child-centered approach for teaching, emphasizing a noncompetitive environment, variety in response, and success for all students, thus fostering social emotional learning and individual worth.
- Aligns with physical education standards and grade-level outcomes or benchmarks.
- Provides assessment strategies within teaching as opposed to drill and test.
- Includes detailed, pertinent safety measures for all lessons of educational gymnastics.
- Provides a wealth of learning experiences, ranging from gymnastics with no equipment to gymnastics using apparatus appropriate for educational gymnastics in the elementary physical education setting.
- Offers learning experiences and assessment strategies for the child-centered, self-responsibility environment of educational gymnastics.

Organization of the Text

Part I of the text, chapters 1 through 3, presents the theoretical background for educational gymnastics. Chapter 1 begins with a comparison of educational and traditional gymnastics. In the United States, our exposure to gymnastics has been the Olympic style. Children at an early age enroll in after-school gymnastics programs and dream of excellence in the competitive world. Perfect execution of each skill is what is rewarded. In contrast, educational gymnastics is child-centered, noncompetitive, and focused on the individual. Learning experiences are designed to meet children at their skill level and expand skills within their level of competence. Laban's Movement Analysis Framework is introduced with a brief explanation of the four categories: body awareness, space awareness, effort, and relationships. Educational gymnastics has a focus on the affective domain for children in the physical education environment; respect for self and others is a major component of daily lessons. This aspect is extremely important in a discipline where self-excellence and competition are highly rewarded. This theoretical base is the foundation for educational gymnastics and the components of balance and weight transfer learning experiences in our elementary physical education programs.

Chapter 2 of the text establishes balance, not just as the core of educational gymnastics but also as the foundation for all movement—within physical education and within life itself. Balance is a key component of gymnastics, sports, and dance. In games and sports the specifics of most individual skills stem from a solid foundation of balance. In dance and gymnastics, balance is the prerequisite to all transfers and travels. Balance is important not only in the world of physical education but also throughout life, from the toddler attempting to stand and take steps to the older person attempting to maintain balance to prevent falls. Balance is the foundation of all movement.

Chapter 3 describes, in theory and practice, a child-centered approach to curriculum and teaching. The chapter emphasizes how teachers and students share the responsibility for making learning occur. Self-responsibility and student success are the primary focus of the child-centered approach. Organization of the teaching environment, legal liability in gymnastics, and safety are among the components presented, including descriptions and examples of each. Teachers need to have a grasp of the child-centered approach presented in this chapter before continuing with part II.

Part II of the text presents the learning experiences that help children develop a functional understanding of the components of educational gymnastics. Chapter 4 establishes Laban's Movement Analysis Framework as the basis of all movement learning and expands, with direct application to gymnastics, the components of the Movement Analysis Framework introduced in chapter 1. The importance of the skills of balance, weight transfer, and travel are established in this chapter. Skills and concepts are introduced with the goal of developing a functional understanding of each, aligned with the Movement Analysis Framework. Teachers should confirm that students demonstrate a functional understanding before they introduce the learning experiences in the remaining chapters.

Chapter 5 focuses on the foundational skill of balance, beginning with the concepts of balance followed by combining balance with the movement concepts learned in chapter 4. Chapter 6 progresses with more challenging balance experiences combined with weight transfer between balances and weight transfers using in-flight actions. The chapter ends with individual and partner sequences. Chapter 7 includes learning experiences on educational gymnastics equipment. Individual and partner sequences on equipment as well as learning experiences on the balance beam, a common gymnastics apparatus, are explored.

The learning experiences in each chapter are presented as a progression based on the development of children both physically and cognitively. The progression is from simple to complex, and the authors suggest you teach in this order. One experience is often a prerequisite to another. Each series of learning experiences is preceded by a cognitive focus, a skill focus, criteria for quality, safety information, and equipment and organization to maximize participation and learning. Challenges are presented throughout the progressions. The challenges can be used when teachers determine that individual students are ready to apply what they have learned. Advanced challenges have been added for the highly skilled students. Each learning experience includes the tasks and safety factors (noted with an icon). Teaching tips are aligned with learning experiences in each chapter.

Educational gymnastics is student centered with a focus on adding to the variety and quality of movements for each child. Encouraging variety helps children increase their body awareness, range of skills, and confidence. Variety also means that students can respond in more than one way to the learning experience. A focus on quality is needed to improve the efficiency of the movement and to ensure safety. The criteria listed in the learning experiences pertain to the quality of the movements. Throughout every lesson, both variety and quality should be emphasized.

Part III of the text contains only one chapter, but it is an important one because it addresses significant questions: "What is your goal for the children you teach, and how do you know they have accomplished that goal?" As teachers of educational gymnastics plan for each day, considering skills, cognitive understanding, and affective learning, their planning is not complete until they address the following question: "What will the children know and be able to do?" Physical education is not recess, nor is it physical activity. Although both are important for children, physical education is a discipline aligned to state and national standards, a discipline that has objectives for each lesson, each unit, each child. The assumption cannot be made that learning has taken place; teachers cannot provide a subjective response to what the child knows and is able to do. Assessment, both formative and summative, is therefore essential to address the issue of learning. Chapter 8 addresses standards and assessment for educational gymnastics.

The eight chapters of *Educational Gymnastics for Children* are written with a belief in balance as the foundation of all movement and educational gymnastics as part of physical education for all children. The text combines the content of educational gymnastics and the teaching strategies of a child-centered curriculum to provide quality programs of educational gymnastics for children.

From the Authors

The authors' introduction to educational gymnastics came early in their teaching careers. Because Shirley's teaching career started first, we begin with her.

My appreciation for the British system of physical education, both curriculum and teaching style, began when I did a summer study in England and observed in their primary and junior schools. I was fascinated with gymnastics and was eager to learn more about the noncompetitive approach to gymnastics and a teaching style that was more student centered than teacher driven. I understood that games and sports are different "across the pond" and was satisfied that creative dance is one avenue within the vast world of dance. But isn't gymnastics supposed to mirror the Olympic style of skills and routines that lead to competition and excellence in performance?

What I observed was gymnastics that was the teaching of skills, based on the work of Rudolf Laban and his analysis of all movement. I saw children balanced on body parts and in configurations that did not resemble anything I had ever seen in Olympic-style gymnastics. Students balanced, transferred weight, and traveled in a variety of ways, some of which resembled the actions of traditional gymnastics, but others that went well beyond those skills and movements.

What was even more impressive than the balances and actions of the students was the absence of off-task behavior and the acceptance of self-responsibility that each student displayed. Each child appeared to be working with full attention to the task they were given, and each appeared to be working differently. Although a common thread appeared throughout the work, students worked at different skill levels, seemingly content and without comparison with others. This style of teaching, I learned, was the child-centered approach—not limiting the highly skilled while not pushing the extremely low skilled with unsafe expectations. After purchasing every book available on educational gymnastics, I returned home eager to begin the new school year with this curriculum and this teaching style as my personal approach to gymnastics.

A decade later, as a senior in college, Tina arrived at the same conclusion after attending a summer workshop led by Shirley and experiencing educational gymnastics. This is Tina's story.

When I began my teaching career, I continued to read and attend state and national conference sessions and summer workshops to learn more about educational gymnastics. I was lucky to work for one year with a colleague who had previously been exposed to the British system. We were able to coteach and explore the child-centered approach to educational gymnastics and dance.

I played many sports and games with my brother and the neighborhood children growing up. Later, thanks to Title IX, I played high school basketball, softball, volleyball, and tennis. Gymnastics was not a part of my childhood. In my university teacher education program, the required gymnastics course was Olympic style, and despite the efforts of a quality instructor, I did not enjoy attending the class. I did not have the skill set or the comfort zone to attempt the challenges presented to us. Had I not been exposed to educational gymnastics, I probably would have avoided teaching gymnastics to my elementary students. I did not think that my training was adequate to teach Olympic-style gymnastics safely. I have heard this same sentiment from many physical educators. I am grateful I was exposed to the child-centered, high-success-rate approach of educational gymnastics. It became my favorite content to teach, and the children were always excited to see the mats out in the gym.

After a combined 56 years of teaching elementary physical education and thousands of students later, Shirley and I are still convinced that educational gymnastics and a child-centered approach to teaching is what is appropriate for children in our elementary physical education programs. We adopted a belief in educational gymnastics for children early in our professional careers and are happy to share that belief with you in this text, *Educational Gymnastics for Children*.

Tina   *Shirley*

ACKNOWLEDGMENTS

The authors want to acknowledge Scott Wikgren for his dedication to physical education. We met Scott in Estes Park, Colorado, at the first ever National Physical Education Conference. His enthusiasm and love of our profession was evident. Scott has worked with and helped countless physical educators over the years. We value his work ethic, his friendship, and his standard for excellence.

The authors want to share our appreciation for the Human Kinetics staff for believing in the future of educational gymnastics for children, for respecting our views on gymnastics for children, and for taking a chance on our "different" format for publication of this book for physical education teachers.

PART I
Foundation of Educational Gymnastics

Educational Gymnastics

Educational gymnastics is balance, weight transfer, and travel. When we think of gymnastics, we typically think of the Olympic gymnast with a slender, muscular body and almost unbelievable skill and strength. We also envision parallel bars, rings, pommel horses, and vaults for men and uneven bars, balance beams, floor routines, and vaults for women. Watching these events causes both excitement and anxiety as the spectacular movements can take your breath away. This is the world of traditional gymnastics. It is a world of precision, in which quality is defined by perfect execution of the skills.

Not so for educational gymnastics. In educational gymnastics there can be as many responses as there are students in the class. Figure 1.1 illustrates this idea with balances on feet and hands. Educational gymnastics is open to all students, regardless of body type, size, or skill. With open-ended tasks and teaching by invitation, each child responds at their individual skill level, meeting the criteria of the task presented.

Whereas safety is a major concern for teachers of physical education, teaching educational gymnastics is as safe as teaching dance and game skills. Child-centered, developmentally appropriate learning experiences and a safe learning environment established by the teacher are at the core of all physical education for children. Part of that safe learning environment includes teaching students not to attempt a movement beyond their individual limitations. Spotters are not used in educational gymnastics; children are taught from the beginning that they are responsible for themselves.

Child-Centered Gymnastics

The teaching of educational gymnastics is not directed to the elite athlete, nor is average the standard for excellence. Child-centered teaching is designed to meet each child where they are and move them beyond that level to the highest level possible for that individual in response to the given task. Children come to physical education "to think, feel and do" (Mauldon and Layson 1965, xi). To think, to feel, to do—cognitive, affective, physical—these are the learning domains of physical education; this is the teaching of children in our gymnasiums and on our playgrounds.

An elementary physical education class of educational gymnastics may be described as organized chaos. A visitor may see what appears, at first glance, as each student doing their own thing. The observer wonders what the focus of the lesson is or even if there is a

FIGURE 1.1   Balancing on feet and hands.

> ## Elite Gymnasts in Physical Education
>
> Traditional Olympic-style gymnastics is not the gymnastics of educational gymnastics. The skills of Olympic-style gymnastics are not the skills of elementary physical education. If you have students in your classes that are in after-school club gymnastics, talk with them in private about the differences and the importance of displaying those skills in their after-school programs, not in physical education classes. They will understand and respect your decision.

focus. Students appear to be working on different tasks. Some are working alone, others with partners. Some are working on planks, some on taped lines on the floor; others are on ladders, bars, and balance beams. Some are engaged in drawings and written work. Where is the teacher? They are not standing in front of the class. They are not requiring everyone to be doing the same skill.

Further observation of the class would reveal each student fully concentrating on their movement skill, either practicing the same skill repeatedly, engaged in refinement of the movements, or adding new movements to the existing skill. Just as the classroom teacher has students working at different levels in math, so does the physical education teacher. Each child is working within the level of their individual potential with the appropriate challenge for moving to the next level of difficulty. Each student appears to know the physical as well as the cognitive expectations of their response. Although 25 students appear to be working on 25 different responses to a task, each appears to know their limits and is comfortable with the challenges within that potential. The teacher moves freely from student to student with personal attention and overall observation, giving feedback and occasionally stopping the class to give a direction, add clarity, pose a question for everyone, extend a challenge, or give a focus for refinement. Then the learning continues.

Laban's Movement Analysis Framework

The curriculum for educational gymnastics centers on the work of Rudolf Laban. Laban was born in 1879 in Hungary. From an early age he was fascinated by the art and the science of movement. He became a student of ballet, a noted choreographer, and a researcher into movement of the human body. He became Director of Movement for the Berlin State Opera then fled the Nazi regime, moving to Britain. During World War II he studied efficiency of movement, applying those principles to industry and later to therapy, as well as to drama, theatre, and dance. His work in the world of dance was the inspiration for the Laban Art of Movement Guild in Great Britain. His notation system for movement in dance is known throughout the world.

The practical application of Laban's study of human movement is an important base for the movement of children in physical education. Laban's Movement Analysis Framework is the foundation, both physically and cognitively, for educational gymnastics, as well as games and creative dance in elementary physical education (figure 1.2). Termed "movement education" in Great Britain, those who studied abroad quickly returned to the United States eager to adopt, and often adapt, this movement education to the content and teaching of elementary physical education (Stanley 1969, 36-75).

Laban's Movement Analysis Framework of skills and concepts is divided into four categories: body awareness, space awareness, effort, and relationships. Learning experiences for the development of each category can be found in chapter 4.

Body Awareness	Space Awareness	Effort	Relationships
• Whole body: stretch, curl, twist	• Personal space	• Time: sudden, sustained	• Between body parts
• Body parts: alone or in combination; initiating or following; stretching, bending, or twisting; meeting or parting	• General space	• Weight (force): heavy, light	• With objects: manipulative, nonmanipulative
	• Directions in space	• Space: direct, flexible	• With people
	• Levels in space	• Flow: bound, free	
	• Pathways in space		
• Weight bearing: support, balance, transference of weight	• Extensions in space: far, near, large, small		
• Actions: locomotion, elevation, turning			
• Body shapes: round, narrow, wide, twisted			
• Symmetrical, asymmetrical use of the body			

FIGURE 1.2 The Movement Analysis Framework.

Adapted from S. Stanley, *Physical Education: A Movement Orientation*, (Toronto: McGraw-Hill Co. of Canada Limited: 1969).

Body Awareness

Body awareness delineates how the body and body parts can move:

- The total body or body parts can stretch, curl, and twist.
- Body parts can move alone or in combination. They can lead an action.
- Body parts can support the total weight of the body—on hands, shoulders, knees, feet, one foot, head in combination with other body parts, and so on.
- Transfer of weight can be from feet to feet, foot to foot, feet to other body parts, and in combination with a variety of locomotor actions.
- The body can move with a variety of locomotor actions, with jumping and landing, with spins, and with rolls.
- The body can balance and transfer weight with wide, narrow, curled, and twisted shapes.
- Stretching, curling, and twisting can lead to symmetrical and nonsymmetrical shapes.
- The body can travel through the air between points of surface contact, that is, flight in gymnastics: floor to floor, floor to equipment or apparatus, equipment or apparatus to floor. Shapes and actions can be made while the body is in midair, that is, in flight.

Body awareness is the core content for educational gymnastics, as the student explores and masters how the body can move leading from awareness to body control.

Space Awareness

Space awareness defines where the body can move and the actions of the body and body parts within that space.

- Body parts can move in personal (self) space; body management begins in self-space as the child balances and moves within their personal space extending high, low, and to the sides without entering the personal space of others.

- Locomotor actions move the body through general space with feet to feet, foot to foot, feet to other body parts, and other body parts in combination, moving with control of self and awareness of the space and travel of others.

- As the body moves in general space, changes in directions, levels, and pathways may be by personal choice or teacher challenge, each adding new dimensions to the exploration and mastery of the skill.

Gymnastics lessons would not keep children's attention if all work was confined to self-space. The addition of traveling skills and the many components of space awareness adds excitement, challenge, and self-motivation for the child's continued growth.

Space awareness is also a critical factor in establishing a safe learning environment in which children are responsible for themselves and others. This awareness fosters an independent learning environment that maximizes student learning. Safety in educational gymnastics will be emphasized throughout the learning experiences of this text and discussed in detail in chapter 3.

Effort

The *effort* components of the movement framework are often neglected in gymnastics, Although the effort concepts receive a heavy emphasis in the expressive dance context, they are important for execution of movement skills in gymnastics.

- Is the movement sudden or controlled and sustained? Does the learner have a choice, or is the time (fast, slow, sudden, sustained) dictated by the action?

- Is the movement one that requires a direct movement, or can a creative, flexible movement be used?

- Does the movement necessitate a free-flowing action, such as a transfer of weight from feet to hands to feet, unstoppable from beginning to end? Is the movement one of bound flow that could be stopped at any moment without injury?

- The fast-travel, direct-pathway, explosive takeoff for a transfer of weight to travel onto or over designated equipment requires different effort qualities than the stretching, curling, or twisting into and out of balances.

Challenge and Expansion of Skills

When children are learning to dribble a ball with the hand, demonstration of the critical elements and body management are sufficient for continuing practice, but after they master the skill, children become quickly bored if confined to self-space. The addition of traveling and variety in levels, directions, and pathways adds challenge and fosters continuing practice and expansion of the skill.

Application of the effort components in gymnastics skills, sequences, and routines is an advanced learning experience that includes individual challenges directed by the teacher. Children's understanding, both cognitive and physical, of the effort components, as with all components of the movement framework, is gained through early lessons focused on introduction and awareness of the skill or concept in isolation before application, This development of awareness and ability for the skills and concepts of the movement framework, the focus of physical education for young children, is the prerequisite for the application of those skills and concepts in all gymnastics, games, and dance (see chapter 4).

Relationships

Relationships, as a movement category, includes interactions between and among body parts, objects, and other people. In gymnastics a relationship is present between how body parts are positioned in relation to each other (e.g., beside, behind, between) for travel, elevation, balance, and weight transfers. Relationships in gymnastics extend the student learning beyond self and into the broader realm of relationships with others, with equipment, and with apparatus.

- Relationships between body parts change the dynamics of travel, weight transfers, and the stability of balances.
- Learning experiences can be designed for students to work on the floor, on equipment, and on apparatus.
- Students work alone, with partners, and as members of a group.
- Sequences can be designed for self; for matching, following, and leading a partner; and for matching and contrasting balances and actions within a group.

From the young child's balances on the floor; to the combination of travel, balances, and weight transfers for a sequence; to the advanced gymnast's floor routine for competition, the relationship of body to surface is essential and unique to each individual. The same is true as the student applies gymnastics skills and concepts to equipment and apparatus. The student knows every inch of the balance beam and every curve of the ladder or bar as they combine travel and balances on the equipment or apparatus.

A full program of educational gymnastics can be provided without equipment or apparatus, but the addition of equipment and apparatus provides new exploration and application, increasing the difficulty of the learning experience and the complexity of the task. What was simple when working on a mat on the gymnasium floor or a grassy outdoor area is suddenly difficult as the student attempts the skill on new surfaces, heights, widths, and configurations of equipment.

Educational gymnastics does not require formal equipment or apparatus. The bars and ladders of playground equipment, benches, low tables, and low balance beams can provide the challenges of travel, balance, and weight transference for expansion and complexity of learning experiences. Chapter 7 provides the learning experiences of educational gymnastics applicable to equipment and apparatus.

The Affective in Gymnastics

This expansion beyond the mastery of gymnastics when working alone provides a richness to the learning experiences and expands the affective learning that is essential in all education in such areas as self-worth, respect, and valuing others as students work with partners and in small-group situations.

The Movement Analysis Framework provides the foundation of the world of educational gymnastics. It relies heavily on the movement components of balance, weight transfer, and travel, all leading to body management. The goal of body management is awareness of balance and weight transfer in all movement coupled with the physical ability to execute that awareness in activity. Body management is important in all sports and daily activities. It begins in elementary physical education, in our programs of educational gymnastics.

Foundation of Games, Sports, and Dance

Educational gymnastics can easily be viewed as the foundation for sports in which children engage. The components of body awareness and space awareness are critical to success in all sports. How many times in soccer does the player need both cognitive awareness and physical mastery of pathways and directions? What is the significance of wide, narrow, and twisted body shapes? How important are stretching, twisting, and curling? Is balance important to a soccer player? What about transference of weight? The list of the components of body and space awareness studied in educational gymnastics is lengthy. Add the ball to the preceding skills, and the soccer portrait is complete.

The same analysis can be made for any sport: team, individual, traditional, nontraditional. The components of body and space awareness, that is, body management, are the foundation on which is built the specific manipulative relationship of balls, rackets, bats, and so on.

Dance is not to be excluded; body management is the foundation for the study and performance of dance. Balance, weight transfer, and locomotion, with a heavy emphasis on the effort components and the expressive use of body and space awareness, are the skills introduced to children at the elementary school level and extended into the highest level of dance performance.

Summary

Body management, leading to control in balance, weight transfer, and locomotion, is the foundation of educational gymnastics. Body and space awareness, coupled with the specific skill of the sport, such as dribbling, catching, throwing, and kicking, is the foundation of all sports. Body and space awareness, coupled with the expressive qualities of effort, is the foundation of dance. The importance of educational gymnastics in the elementary physical education curriculum cannot be overstated. It is the foundation of all physical education.

Reflection Questions

1. Contrast traditional and educational gymnastics. Chart, diagram, or describe in written form the differences.
2. What are the categories of the Movement Analysis Framework? Provide an example of each for educational gymnastics.
3. Choose your favorite sport and list the body and space awareness components for that sport.
4. Why is body management considered the foundation of physical education?

References

Mauldon, E., and Layson, J. (1965). *Teaching Gymnastics*. London: Macdonald & Evans.

Stanley, S. (1969). *Physical Education: A Movement Orientation*. Toronto: McGraw-Hill of Canada.

Balance as the Foundation for Movement

Balance, the central component of educational gymnastics and the central component of body management, is not only an essential skill for physical education but also a critical component for a lifetime of wellness. Body management is not confined to our gymnasiums and playgrounds. Its importance is not limited to sports. From the beginning stages of a child's attempts to stand through a lifetime of mobility without falls, balance is critical to life itself.

Balance in Gymnastics

Balance is the foundation of all gymnastics, traditional and educational. When jumping from a low crate or beam, the youngster bends the knees and lowers the hips to land in a balanced position. Gymnasts finish their routines with the "Ta-da"—arms extended upward, shoulders over hips, and hips over feet so that the body is aligned for stability. The Olympic gymnast knows that sticking the landing is a critical component of the routine; the slightest loss of balance results in a reduction of points from the final score.

Early lessons in gymnastics focus on bases of support, wide versus narrow bases, alignment of body parts over the base of support, extensions and counterextensions, and muscular tension. Children explore balance and practice it on the floor and on mats as they develop a working understanding of balance and control of their bodies. Foundational gymnastics skills also include stability in jumping and landing as well as dynamic balance for traveling.

Exploration of low equipment—planks, beams, benches, step boxes, and folded mats—begins with stability. Children maintain and regain balance in travel, single stationary balances, and balanced landings for dismounts. Body management is the focus for the early exploration of gymnastics equipment as children develop responsibility for self and spatial awareness of others.

Brigance Early Childhood Screening

For years one of the tests given to all youngsters preparing to enter kindergarten has been a measure of balance—standing on one foot for five seconds. Fast forward to the present, and those same boys and girls are now classified as senior citizens and reporting to their personal physicians for a wellness checkup. Included in that wellness checkup is a test of balance—standing on one foot for five seconds!

After they gain a working understanding of balance and body control, students are ready for more challenging learning experiences in gymnastics. The foundation expands with a focus on quality. Students explore and practice for mastery of balances on narrower bases of support, the full range of body shapes on each base of support, balances at different levels, and inverted balances. Note: When young children hear the term "inverted balances," they immediately think of headstands, handstands, and advanced skills of inversion. Early lessons focus on the concept of inversion, that is, any balance when the head is lower than the hips (see figure 2.1).

Weight transference moves the student into and out of balances; twisting, curling, and stretching actions are explored as the means for transfers with the focus always on the balance before and after the transfer. Jumping with one-foot and two-foot takeoffs is developed with a match between the action, the landing balance, and the appropriate takeoff.

Combinations of travel and balances lead to sequences. The complexity of action and balance combinations is enhanced with the addition of pathways, directions, and changes in levels to the travel.

The foundational skills introduced in the early learning experiences are practiced and refined with *quality* movement as the goal. Work on low apparatus is now more complex with sequences, approaches, and dismounts as children explore, practice, and master balances onto, on, and off gymnastics equipment and apparatus. Balance is the cornerstone for all gymnastics equipment and apparatus work.

The progression of gymnastics increases the difficulty and challenge of the task. Many of the tasks presented early in gymnastics are repeated with increased variety and complexity in responses from the learner. A simple balance on a chosen body part becomes a challenge with inversion and stillness, with extensions and counterextensions, working with a partner or in a group. The earlier mastery of balanced landings combined with one-foot and two-foot takeoffs provides the basics for the introduction of flight and the many possibilities of shapes and actions while the body is airborne. Gymnastics apparatus and configurations of gymnastics equipment challenge the students, both cognitively and physically, with balances and weight transfers. Sequences become more complex as the student's repertoire of skills and the addition of travel and movement concepts come together at the highest level of potential for each child. That is the goal of educational gymnastics. That is the goal for all teachers of children.

Meeting Individual Student Needs

The progression of student learning experiences in part II of this book is not designed by children's chronological age or by grade levels. Instead, the progression is designed to meet each child where they are in their functional understanding of gymnastics and to provide the appropriate challenges for continued growth toward their potential.

FIGURE 2.1   Inverted balances in early lessons.

Balance in Games and Sports

Ask yourself this question: How many times when learning the skills of a new game or sport were you taught the specifics of balance for that game? If you played on a varsity team, did your coach discuss the importance of balance and stability in the game? Was it just a discussion, or were you taught the principles of balance that specifically related to that game, such as the split step in tennis in readiness for the next hit, the jump stop in basketball to prevent a charging violation, the wide base in preparation for a swing in striking a ball, the jump to catch a high ball in baseball followed by a quick throw to the base upon landing? The how and why are both important for the proper execution of the skill and for success in the game or sport.

Balance is not a naturally occurring skill; the ability to balance, both static and dynamic, is a learned skill. Although generic in its rudimentary form, the ability to balance has specific components for the particular skill being mastered as seen in the preceding examples. Balance is more than not falling down; balance contributes to successful striking, kicking, volleying, dribbling (foot and hand), throwing, catching, all locomotors with changes in direction, pathways, speed, starting and stopping, jumping and landing, offense, defense—all skills, all sports.

The important principles of balance, so necessary for gymnastics, are equally important for games and sports: wide versus narrow base of support, alignment of body parts over base of support, extensions and counterextensions, stability and the recovery of such in dynamic situations. Balance in games and sports leads to body management and control; body control in planned and unplanned situations coupled with cognitive and physical mastery of skills leads to success in games and sports.

Balance in Dance

Balance in gymnastics and in games and sports is often referred to as functional movement, whereas balance in dance, while functional, is expressive in nature. Balance in stillness and travel provide the freedom for the child to focus on the expressive use of the body and body parts to convey the message of the dance. The young child jumps and leaps in the early stages of imagery in movement. The skilled dancer uses those same jumping and leaping skills combined with the repertoire of skills from the Movement Analysis Framework to create an expressive dance as a study of movement components, or to tell a story in movement. The combined travel and stillness require balance at its highest level for the dance to convey the wishes of the dancer—both the youngster in our elementary schools and the ballet dancer on the Metropolitan stage. Balance is the prerequisite for all dance skills and as such provides the body management for the dancer to create the illusion of a body suspended in space, moving between travel and stillness in total freedom yet in control at all times.

Balance in sports and dance.
Photos courtesy of the authors.

Balance as a Lifetime Skill

Balance and muscular strength are necessary for the young child to sit, to stand, and to walk. Stability in motion and in stillness is needed for hopping, galloping, and skipping. Balance is tested as the young child walks on curbs and climbs on everything—chairs, trees, ladders, backyard swings, and playground bars. Balance is essential for hopscotch, learning to ride a bike, jumping rope, and skating. Confidence in the ability to maintain and regain balance leads to new challenges and the young child's mastery of their world. Confidence in movement skills for young children leads to increased physical activity in adolescents and a willingness to try new activities, such as skateboarding, snowboarding, paddleboarding, skiing, surfing, equestrian riding, diving, and kayaking.

Little thought is given to balance in adults as they pursue their careers and recreational activities. Wide bases of support, alignment of body parts over the base, and the ability to regain balance happen with little conscious thought. A focus on the ability to maintain and regain balance rises to the front when older family members are suddenly facing issues of stability and decreasing mobility.

Observation of older adults shows a shortened stride in walking with cautious movement rather than forward movement with a normal-length stride. Conversation with those adults will reveal a fear of falling. This fear and loss of confidence lead to a decrease in physical activity, leading to a decline in mobility. This downward spiral has major health consequences. Muscular strength and balance are greatly affected, social interactions diminish, and feelings of loneliness lead to depression. Balance is a key factor in physical and emotional fitness and wellness throughout the lifespan; it is *the* key factor for older adults.

Summary

Balance is not confined to gymnastics; it is not limited in scope to the physical education curriculum. The ability to maintain and regain balance in planned and unplanned situations leads to confidence in movement and to safety in that movement. The body control that comes from balance opens doors for increased physical activity, for fitness, wellness, and quality of life. It is the foundation for movement.

Reflection Questions

1. Why is balance referred to as a lifetime skill?
2. Choose one balance component (e.g., wide base of support, alignment of body parts over the base, extensions and counterextensions) and describe its use in five sports.
3. Compare and contrast balance in games, gymnastics, and dance.

Photo courtesy of the authors.

Establishing the Teaching and Learning Environment for Educational Gymnastics

A positive and productive teaching and learning environment is critical to success in physical education. Teachers and students are both responsible for making learning occur. The teacher must design and build a positive learning environment. The students, while engaged physically and cognitively, are expected to stay on task and work safely and productively.

Child-Centered Approach

Educational gymnastics is a child-centered approach to teaching in which the teacher meets each child at their skill level and then guides the individual to move beyond with expectations to meet full potential. In essence, the teacher leads the students to recognize their unique abilities and discover what they can do with those abilities. The child-centered approach uses indirect instruction. The teacher gives a task to the class and then encourages individual responses as students explore and discover their responses to the task (figure 3.1). With this independent process, students become highly engaged and responsible in the learning process as exploration, discovery, decision making, and creativity are encouraged. Initially, this approach may be challenging for both teachers and children. The physical education specialist, because of training and personal experiences, is often more comfortable using a direct style of teaching wherein they present a task and expect all students to respond in a specific manner. This would be more of a whole-class approach (figure 3.2). At the same time, the independent-learning approach may be a new experience for children that results in apprehension or uncertainty about teacher expectations and past experiences of seeking the right answer.

FIGURE 3.1   Child-centered approach.

FIGURE 3.2   Whole-class approach.

When children adapt to this type of learning, and they quickly do, it is fascinating to observe their concentration while discovering what their bodies can do. With child-centered educational gymnastics experiences, the results are self-responsibility, an increase in body control, a rich repertoire of balances and weight transfers, and the ability to refine actions to achieve full potential.

Self-Responsibility and Student Success

The child-centered approach to teaching educational gymnastics requires the child to exhibit self-responsibility. The goal is for students to take ownership in decision making and to move with a clear focus on body control and safety, for self and others. With clear teacher expectations along with encouragement and experience, students will become more competent and confident in the role of responsible active learners.

Success-Oriented Learning Environment

The teacher must promote student ownership and encourage children to work at individual levels of ability. Students are never put in a position where they are pressured to attempt tasks for which they are not ready. The teacher encourages the child to progress when ready. Creativity is fostered, and children are encouraged to find value and self-satisfaction in their individual movement abilities. With time, students develop the tools to create and make their movement responses unique to their abilities and creativity. Requiring students to engage in thoughtful control of their body's movements, providing feedback with a focus on personal improvement, and allowing each child to progress at their levels creates a learning environment that is success oriented.

Prerequisites for Individual Success

Student success in physical education is typically measured by what students know and are able to do—the assessment of skills and knowledge. As stated earlier, the child-centered approach of educational gymnastics involves guiding children beyond their current skill levels to help them reach their potential. The result is the acquisition of new skills and knowledge. Prerequisite skills and knowledge, however, play a part in a child's potential for success.

Foundational Skills and Knowledge

Chapter 4, Movement Analysis Framework, provides the groundwork for preparing students for quality educational gymnastics experiences. They must have a functional understanding of the movement concepts under the broad categories of body awareness, space awareness, effort, and relationships. In other words, they must have both knowledge of the concepts and the ability to demonstrate the actions. Additionally, students should be able to accurately perform locomotor skills and the foundational skills of jumping and landing. The functional understanding of the movement concepts, locomotor skills, and jumping and landing are the prerequisites for students to be successful in the learning experiences of chapters 5 through 7.

Individual Differences

Children come to physical education in all sizes, body shapes, and ability levels. These differences, along with their varied movement experiences out of school, create the challenge of meeting individual needs. You may have students in your classes who participate in club gymnastics after school and have achieved an advanced skill level of gymnastics.

Teacher demonstrates and asks the students to focus on stillness.
Photo courtesy of the authors.

You will have students who are lacking in skill-related fitness components such as strength, flexibility, and balance. Strength, flexibility, and balance influence a person's potential in many gymnastics learning experiences. Your students will differ in body size. Size and weight of children, including how weight is proportioned, vary and may influence student success. For example, children who carry a lot of weight in the midsection may not have the strong core needed for advanced balances. On the other hand, an exceptionally thin child may not have the upper-body strength needed to take weight on hands long enough to transfer weight with good extensions.

As the learning experiences in chapters 6 and 7 become more challenging, prerequisite physical abilities may be more obvious. Educational gymnastics, however, allows all students to experience success. Unique physical characteristics and abilities further promote the need for the child-centered approach, meeting each child at their skill level and moving beyond to meet their potential. Children must never be put in a position where they cannot succeed because of lack of prerequisite skills or physical abilities.

In chapters 5 through 7, we have labeled some learning experiences as challenges and some as advanced challenges. The teacher needs to determine which students are ready to progress while encouraging others to continue working on previous or alternate tasks. Many students will be ready for the challenges, but only the highly skilled should be encouraged to attempt the advanced challenges. With the child-centered approach, students learn to respect and appreciate that the teacher is guiding them in reaching their individual goals instead of comparing them with other students.

Instruction Using a Child-Centered Approach

The child-centered, indirect teaching approach and the direct approach used by most physical educators have similarities in teacher instruction. Both have the goal of quality outcomes and skillful movers. Both require teachers to provide effective task presentations, demonstrations with clear expectations, observation of student performance, feedback, assessment, review from previous work, and when possible distributed practice (revisiting skills throughout the theme, module, unit, or year).

Although the two teaching approaches have similarities in instruction, the differences are notable. The teacher expectation of the student response to a task is perhaps what differs the most. With the child-centered approach, the teacher encourages a variety of responses while at the same time expecting quality in the child's movement. Comparing the direct teaching of a V-sit balance and the indirect teaching of balancing on different bases of support illustrates the differences. In traditional gymnastics a teacher would provide specific learning cues and demonstrations of exactly how to perform the V-sit skill. The end goal would be balancing on the seat with legs extended in straddle position, using tight core muscles. An initial expectation may be to include the hands for added support and choose pike or straddle position. In contrast, when teaching balancing on a variety of bases of support, the teacher is inviting the students to create and discover an array of balances. The demonstrations and cues will focus on the qualities of stillness, muscular tension, alignment, and use of free body parts for extension or counterbalance. The end goal is for the students to demonstrate those qualities in a repertoire of balances on different bases of support, in different shapes, and at high, medium, and low levels. An initial expectation would be to explore different bases of support with a focus on holding the balance still for three to five seconds.

At first, children with few experiences in gymnastics or the indirect teaching approach may struggle to produce a response. To aid in this process, early in the learning experiences we suggest that teachers guide students through a few specific examples before encouraging them to explore other options. Student success in exploration varies. Some need more guidance and suggestions, whereas others work well independently. During exploration, avoid implying that a single option is best. Encourage students to work within their comfort zones. Although you may pinpoint children who are showing the quality of an inverted balance (i.e., stillness, muscular tension, alignment), do not imply that the chosen base of support is what you expect of all. To avoid this, pinpoint several students who are demonstrating quality but using different bases of support (figure 3.3).

When presenting the tasks, ask students to explore two or three options and then expand when they are ready. Avoid asking, "How many ways . . . ?" because some children may think they have failed if they can come up with only one. Another common question to avoid is, "Can you . . . ?" because the reply may be, "No, I can't," and then the student will make no attempt to explore. For students to have a variety of responses, provide numerous practice opportunities before moving on to a new task. For example, say, "Continue exploring different bases of support at a low level until you hear the signal to stop."

FIGURE 3.3   Pinpointing students with quality extensions and tight muscles.

Exploration and discovery take time. As students gain experience, they may take longer to respond to a task. They have expanded their movement repertoire and are refining their work. Quality and variety take time for all students. Embrace it and be patient.

The learning experiences in chapters 5 through 7 focus on variety in student responses and the quality of their balances and weight transfers. Encouraging variety will help children increase their range of skills, body awareness, and confidence in their creativity. The focus on quality is needed to improve both the efficiency of their balances and weight transfers and safety. Each learning experience in chapters 5 through 7 provides a skill outcome, cognitive focus, and criteria for success. Figure 3.4 illustrates a sample learning experience introduction from chapter 5. Combined, they provide the focus on quality needed for teacher observation, feedback, and student engagement.

Time, Space, and Equipment Constraints

Time, space, and equipment will influence the learning experiences that a teacher can provide for educational gymnastics. Physical education may take place in a gymnasium, a multipurpose room, a cafeteria, a hallway, or outdoors. Some schools may have an abundance of gymnastics equipment, whereas others may be limited. Mats are typically available, but the type and number vary. Mats may be large with three or four folds or small, lightweight individual mats.

Time is probably the number one influence in deciding what to teach. Students may attend physical education as seldom as once a week to as often as daily. If time with students is limited, doing fewer of the learning experiences is better than rushing through them. Review will also be necessary. The decision to move on is based on the teacher's observation of student responses to tasks, not a preplanned number of minutes. When most students meet teacher expectations for variety and quality, it is time to progress. Planning decisions will be influenced by time, space, and equipment, but limitations require adaptation and flexibility, not elimination of educational gymnastics experiences for children.

Organizing the Learning Environment

When teaching educational gymnastics, the teacher must arrange the learning environment to maximize participation and minimize wait time. Children should not be stand-

---

Balancing Shapes and Levels

Cognitive: Balances can be in wide, narrow, curled, twisted, symmetrical, and nonsymmetrical shapes. A wide base of support is more stable. Balances can be at low, medium, or high levels. Base of support, levels, and body shapes combine to make a variety of balances. Use decision-making skills to meet the criteria required.

Skills: Perform quality balances on different bases of support, at different levels, and with a variety of body shapes.

Criteria: Tight muscles, alignment, and stillness.

Safety: Personal space. Ensure that mats (if used) do not slide.

Equipment and organization: No equipment or individual small mats; students in personal space. Paper and pencil for each child.

FIGURE 3.4   Sample learning experience introduction.

ing in long lines taking turns on mats or equipment. The mats should be organized for individual use or for sharing. Figure 3.5 demonstrates options for safely sharing mats. Ideally, no more than two students should be using the same mat, although having a limited number of mats may require three students to share a large mat.

The organization of the mats should be taken into consideration. First, ensure that mats are well spaced, allowing students to work safely without interfering with others. Second, the mats should be organized so that the teacher can move, observe, and provide feedback while still observing other students for safe, on-task behavior. Third, develop a clear plan of the procedure for students to share space on a mat or take turns. Lack of mats may limit choices of the learning experiences in educational gymnastics. Safety should never be compromised because of a lack of mats.

Gymnastics Stations

If sufficient mats are not available, an option is the use of stations. Chapter 7, Educational Gymnastics With Equipment, is designed using stations. Station teaching requires planning the organization of equipment, rotation pattern, signal to stop in preparation to rotate, time at each station, and the way in which equipment is shared within a station. Safety rules should be posted at each station and brought to the attention of students daily. Some learning experiences may require posting the various tasks at each station. A common error in teaching with stations is to spend long periods at the beginning of class informing students of expectations at each station. The children are eager to go and are not likely to absorb much information. As you will see in chapter 7, most tasks are the same, but the equipment varies. The idea is to explore the many challenges that different pieces of equipment offer. Each learning experience provides a focus, and with the child-centered approach that includes discovery, creativity, skill enhancement, and decision making.

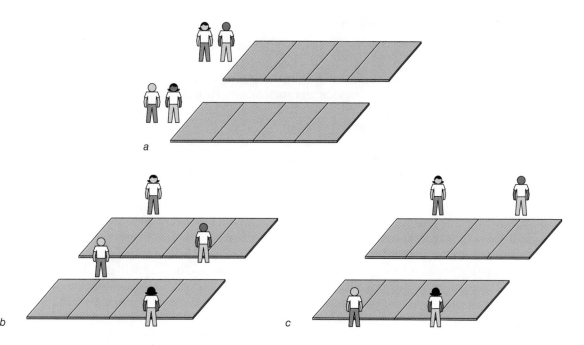

FIGURE 3.5   Options for safely sharing mats include *(a)* lengthwise and taking turns, *(b)* widthwise and facing the opposite direction, and *(c)* widthwise and facing the same direction.

Recording Balances and Transfers

When children begin to create balances and weight transfers with rotation to different pieces of equipment or stations, they can easily forget what actions they did and where, especially when the stations are continued from one class period to the next. We have found that written recording in the form of stick figures not only aids in recall but also helps promote variety as children work at the different stations. They can simply record their balances and weight transfers on a blank piece of paper. Students can add their name and homeroom, or the teacher may choose to use a prepared worksheet that can also serve as an assessment. Figure 3.6 is a sample prepared worksheet for recording balances and transfers on equipment. The worksheets used for recording are also beneficial when children begin to develop sequences. The method for recording information, the responsibility for worksheets as children rotate stations, and the storage of worksheets can be done in several ways. Some teachers find it best to have a designated area where students go to record their work, with worksheets and pencils remaining in that designated area. Others have found it best for students to take worksheets with them as they change stations, leaving pencils at each station. Teachers can collect worksheets as students leave at the end of class, students can file worksheets in their individual portfolios, or students can leave worksheets in a designated area. You as the teacher will quickly determine what works best for your teaching environment; the students will quickly accept the responsibility for their worksheets.

Safe Learning Environments

Many teachers report that they do not teach gymnastics because of fear that a student will be hurt. Some have shared that their school or district administrators do not allow gymnastics because of concerns of safety and legal liability. We share the same concerns with traditional, or Olympic-style, gymnastics.

Prevention of Legal Liability

Legal liability in teaching requires proof of negligence. According to the Merriam-Webster dictionary, negligence is defined as "the failure to exercise the care that a reasonably prudent person would use under the circumstances involved."

Negligence in physical education is preventable when teachers supervise activity well, inform students of safety protocols and enforce their use, and ensure that all equipment is safe. Physical education supervision requires teachers to position themselves where all students are in sight. Unlike in the classroom, any distraction, such as a teacher taking a phone call, viewing a text, or stopping to speak to another teacher or administrator, often requires students to stop activity momentarily. Informing students of safety protocols and reinforcing the expectations are ongoing in the active, moving environment of physical education. The lesson introduction should include any safety precautions for the day. Throughout the lesson, the teacher observes for safety, reinforces good safety practice, and immediately intervenes if a child's action is unsafe. The child-centered approach relies on both the teacher and the students to maintain a safe learning environment. This combination promotes independent learning for students and quality skill development.

Teachers are responsible for ensuring that all equipment is safe. Educational gymnastics equipment such as boxes, tables, and benches should be checked for sturdiness and to ensure they do not slide when a child jumps on or off the equipment. Equipment purchased specifically for gymnastics, such as those discussed in chapter 7, should be checked for sturdiness and to ensure that each piece is used according to industry standards (Werner, Williams, and Hall 2012). Mats should be placed beside or under equipment and positioned for landing when coming off the equipment (figure 3.7). Equipment should never be left

Name: _Jane O._   Classroom Teacher: _Ms. Ball_

Learning experience focus: Create a series of three balances at three different levels, with travel between each. Make it your best before recording with stick figures below.

Equipment Choice #1:

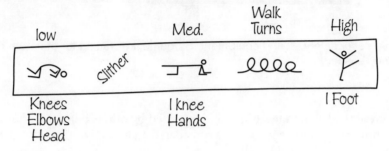

Equipment Choice #2:

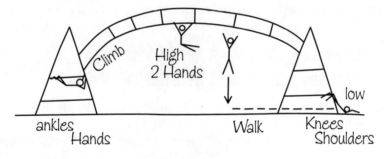

Respond to the following questions:

1. How did the equipment change from choice #1 to choice #2 influence your choices of balances?

   Bases of support changed, easier on bench.

2. How did the equipment change from choice #1 to choice #2 influence your choices of levels?

   High level more fun on #2.

3. How did the equipment change from choice #1 to choice #2 influence your choices of travel?

   I could climb on 2, slither on 1. Two was more fun.

FIGURE 3.6   Sample recording worksheet.

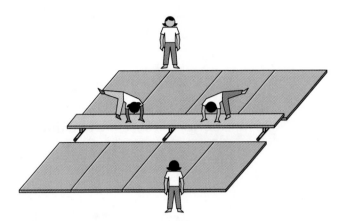

FIGURE 3.7   Mats for safety around equipment. Students are waiting for their turn clearly out of working space.

out if the physical education teaching facility is used by others before or after school. If someone is hurt, the equipment could be considered an attractive nuisance. The result is possible injury as well as legal liability.

In educational gymnastics, if the learning environment is established with an emphasis on teaching body control, self-responsibility, and safe practices, the benefits are endless, and the learning experiences are as safe as those in other physical education learning experiences.

Safety Expectations and Student Self-Responsibility

Part of creating the safe learning environment is teaching for safety and self-responsibility. Teachers must instruct students on safety expectations and protocols and revisit and reinforce their use. Self-responsibility specific to safety includes the following suggestions:

- Safely move in and out of all movements. Always know your safe exit from an inverted balance or weight transfer and always have a safe exit off equipment.
- When you hear the stop signal, finish your movement, and come to a rest. (An abrupt stop can be dangerous in gymnastics.)
- Always use space awareness; be aware of others and ready to adjust your movement in relation to others if necessary. When on equipment, you may be under, on top, or inverted on the piece of equipment. Be aware of others on the same equipment.
- When jumping, always land under control on two feet.
- Never assist or spot others. Spotting encourages students to attempt skills they are not ready to try. Spotting can be dangerous for both the student spotting and the one being spotted. Educational gymnastics promotes self-responsibility, not spotting.
- Never work in sock feet. Bare feet or shoes are required. (Bare feet are best for quality movement in gymnastics, but many schools or school districts do not allow children to be shoeless.)
- Do not copy the work of others. Work within the limits of your ability and with all movements under control.
- Never distract another person by touching or speaking to them when they are involved in gymnastics work. Full concentration is needed for safety of self and others.

Safe practices for teachers include always observing for safety. After presenting a task, the first observation should be to ensure that all students are working safely. Then, throughout the practice time, the teacher should be positioned to have all students in view while continuing to observe for safety and on-task behavior in addition to providing individual feedback and challenges. The use of a safety check in educational gymnastics has proved to be effective in preventing unsafe practices. Any time you observe an unsafe practice, give a signal and announce, "Safety check." Students should be taught to complete their movement, come to a stop, and assume listening position. Safety checks are typically used when there is evidence of off-task behaviors or a lack of space awareness that could result in the endangerment of self or others.

For some learning experiences, specific safety concerns must be provided to students. In chapters 4 through 7, we have brought these to your attention by using a safety icon. For example, when teaching the forward safety roll, emphasis must be placed on keeping the chin tucked to roll safely and taking no weight on the head. In chapter 7, several precautions are presented regarding use of equipment. As stated earlier, the teacher begins by placing mats beside and under the equipment and in position for dismounting off the equipment. Each piece of equipment has specific safety protocols to bring to the students' attention.

Summary

Educational gymnastics is open to all students regardless of skill, body type, or size. Educational gymnastics uses a child-centered approach wherein students are highly engaged and exhibit self-responsibility. Some teachers may have to step out of their comfort zone to guide students in the child-centered learning experiences of educational gymnastics. With time, many teachers discover, as we have, that gymnastics is their favorite content to teach. We know from experience that gymnastics is a favorite of children. Although safety is a major concern for teachers in traditional gymnastics, educational gymnastics does not present significant safety concerns. It is as safe as any other physical education learning experience. With a safe learning environment, where children practice self-responsibility and know that the focus is on their success instead of comparison with others, children will find great joy in discovering, exploring, and creating balances and weight transfers both on the mats and on equipment.

Reflection Questions

1. Explain why a functional understanding of the movement concepts is the foundation for educational gymnastics.

2. Select three examples of movement concepts and explain the importance of functional understanding with application to gymnastics.

3. Compare and contrast direct teaching with the indirect teaching used in the child-centered approach of educational gymnastics.

4. Share three ways that a teacher can ensure safety in the educational gymnastics learning environment.

References

Werner, P.H., Williams, L.H., and Hall, T.J. 2012. *Teaching Children Gymnastics*. 3rd ed. Champaign, IL: Human Kinetics.

PART II

Learning Experiences in Educational Gymnastics

Movement Analysis Framework

The Movement Analysis Framework, developed by Rudolph Laban, contains all the skills and concepts of human movement and, as such, contains all the skills and concepts of elementary physical education: games, dance, gymnastics (see figure 1.2 in chapter 1). The *skills* of educational gymnastics are balance, weight transference, locomotion (travel), elevation (jumping and landing), and the actions of stretching, curling, and twisting. The movement *concepts* of the framework are the cognitive categories of body awareness, space awareness, effort, and relationships, as introduced in chapter 1.

A functional understanding of the movement concepts and the skills of traveling, jumping and landing, and the actions of twisting, curling, and stretching are the prerequisites to children's work in balance and weight transference. A cognitive understanding and the ability to move with that understanding is essential in educational gymnastics. For example, asking children to balance on different bases of support will be difficult if they do not understand the term or the body parts capable of being bases of support. The intent is for the movement vocabulary to become the "academic language" for the physical education teacher and students.

Teaching the Concepts and Prerequisites

For teachers of elementary physical education, the focus of our lessons is on student learning; for children, the focus is movement. Children come to physical education to move. They travel on their feet and on various body parts. They travel in different directions and at different levels. They run, they jump, they hop, they creep, they crawl. Movement is the young child's mode of learning; it is the joy of the day for children in our elementary schools. Our task is to build on that natural movement with the learning experiences to expand, refine, and enrich that learning. That task requires the foundation of movement concepts and skills.

Observation of children in their natural world of movement reveals the importance of the early movement skills and movement concepts. We quickly recognize that the teaching of the movement concepts may or may not be in the order in which they are listed on the Movement Analysis Framework. The order of the learning experiences presented in this chapter does not imply a hierarchy or developmental sequence. All are interrelated; teachers can build what they see as a logical order. Figure 4.1 shows the movement concepts of the framework with an irregular pattern.

The introductory learning experiences presented in this chapter, coupled with child-centered teaching, will provide the functional understanding of the Movement Analysis Framework that will serve as the foundation for educational gymnastics. In their generic form, the skills and concepts are applicable to all areas of physical education with specific learning experiences for gymnastics, games, and dance (figure 4.2). The movement concepts are the foundation of all learning in physical education. In gymnastics they are followed by the basic skills of locomotion, balance, weight transference, and the actions

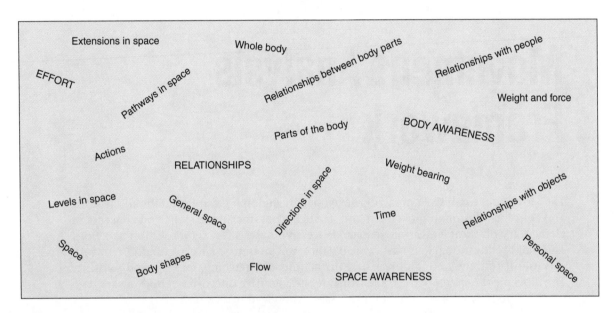

FIGURE 4.1 Movement Analysis Framework concepts.

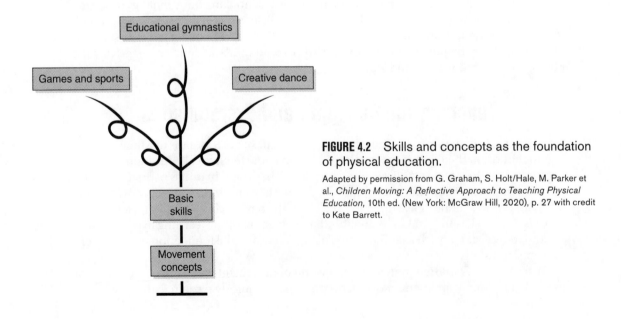

FIGURE 4.2 Skills and concepts as the foundation of physical education.

Adapted by permission from G. Graham, S. Holt/Hale, M. Parker et al., *Children Moving: A Reflective Approach to Teaching Physical Education*, 10th ed. (New York: McGraw Hill, 2020), p. 27 with credit to Kate Barrett.

of stretching, curling, and twisting, all of which are built on space awareness and safety for self and others.

The basic skills and the concepts of the movement framework should be taught before children begin the study of gymnastics. The skills and concepts of the framework are the prerequisites for children's work in balance and weight transference. Lesson plans for teaching each of the movement concepts and skills may be found in *Lesson Planning for Elementary Physical Education: Meeting the National Standards and Grade-Level Outcomes* (Holt/ Hale and Hall 2016). Sample lesson plans for the teaching of the concept of body shapes (appendix A) and the skill of jumping and landing (appendix B) can be found at the end of this chapter (Holt/Hale and Hall 2016). The introductory functional understanding of the movement framework, found in this chapter's learning experiences, followed by the development of balance and weight transference in the learning experiences (chapters 5-7) provides the richness of educational gymnastics for all children.

This chapter presents the skills and concepts of the Movement Analysis Framework as an introduction to a functional understanding for their development (see figure 4.3). These prerequisite concepts and skills are needed for student success in gymnastics. Although gymnastics concentrates heavily on the skills of balance and weight transference, all the movement concepts and skills of the framework are integral parts of the educational gymnastics curriculum.

The learning experiences that follow are separated into cognitive (left column) and performance (right column) for the development of a functional understanding. Following each skill or concept, examples from traditional gymnastics actions are used to help the reader who is new to this framework make the concept and skill connection (titled Making the Connection). Detailed educational gymnastics learning experiences for the development and application of the skills and concepts relating to balance and weight transfer are found in chapters 5 through 7.

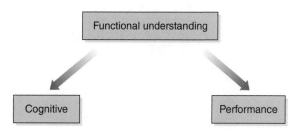

FIGURE 4.3   Functional understanding of skills and concepts.

Mini Index for Learning Experiences

Body Awareness 35
    Whole Body .... .35
    Body Parts .... .36
    Weight Bearing .... .37
    Actions .... .39
    Body Shapes .... .42
Space Awareness 44
    Personal and General Space .... .44
    Directions .... .45
    Levels .... .46
    Pathways .... .47
    Extensions .... .48
Effort 49
    Time .... .49
    Weight (Force) .... .50
    Space .... .50
    Flow .... .51
Relationships 52
    Between Body Parts .... .52
    With Objects .... .53
    With People .... .53

BODY AWARENESS

Body awareness is what the body as a whole can do and how specific body parts can be supportive, moved into different shapes, or used in actions.

Skills

- Whole body
  - Stretch, curl, twist
- Body parts
  - Stretch, bend, twist, initiate, follow, meet, part
- Weight bearing
  - Bases of support, balance, transfer weight
- Actions
  - Locomotion (traveling), elevation (jumping and landing), turning

Concepts

- Body shapes
  - Round, narrow, wide, twisted
  - Symmetrical and asymmetrical

WHOLE BODY

The whole body can stretch, curl, or twist (figure 4.4).

Cognitive	Performance
Stretching is extending the body to its fullest length.	Explore stretching upward until you are fully stretched, to the right, to the left.
	Explore stretching while standing, lying on the floor.
The spine curls; other body parts bend.	Explore curling the spine forward as far as you can curl, to the side.
	🚧 **Carefully curl the spine backward.**
	Explore curling while standing, kneeling, sitting, while lying on your back, your stomach, on one side.
Twisting occurs when the body rotates over a stationary base of support.	Standing on two feet, use your spine to rotate the entire body as far as you can in a twisting motion; stop and twist the other way.
	Explore twisting the whole body while kneeling, sitting, while lying on your back, your stomach, on one side.
	Explore combining the stretching, curling, twisting actions of the spine moving from one to another while standing, kneeling, sitting, while lying on your back, your stomach, on one side.

Making the Connection: A gymnastic weight transfer or balance learning experience may include a stretching, curling, or twisting action of the entire body. Visualize the curling, stretching, or twisting actions of a traditional roll or round-off and the way that the body stretches to extend in a headstand or handstand.

FIGURE 4.4   Stretching, curling, and twisting actions.

BODY PARTS

Body parts alone or in combination can stretch, bend, twist; initiate actions (lead, follow), meet and part.

Cognitive	Performance
Body parts, alone or in combination with other body parts, can stretch, bend, and twist.	While seated in self-space, stretch your legs forward, stretch legs and arms forward. Explore stretching other free body parts while standing, kneeling, lying on your back, on your side.
	Standing on your feet, bend your knees as far as you can while still maintaining your balance.
	Explore bending different body parts while standing, kneeling, lying on your back, on your side.
	Explore twisting body parts while supporting your weight on feet, knees, back, stomach. Remember that the supporting body parts do not move.
Body parts can initiate actions; other body parts follow or meet and part.	Play follow-the-leader in self-space; one body part initiates the movement (lead part), and another body part follows the movement. Explore the lead-and-follow actions while standing, kneeling, sitting, or lying on your back.
	Spread your arms wide apart; bring your hands in slowly to meet each other. Explore other body parts that can meet and part.

Making the Connection: In gymnastics, body parts may stretch, twist, or bend as one moves from one balance into another. Body parts can follow other body parts in the action. For example, hand follows hand to initiate the cartwheel and foot follows foot in galloping.

WEIGHT BEARING

Weight bearing includes bases of support, balance, and weight transference. The body is supported by body parts for all balances, for traveling, and for all weight transfers including the takeoff and landing phases of the body in flight. The following introduce the concepts of base of support, balance, and weight transfer (figure 4.5). Chapters 5 through 7 are dedicated to these experiences.

Cognitive	Performance
Static balance requires body management with the criterion of stillness. The base of support is the body part or parts in contact with the ground and supporting the body.	Explore the body parts, alone and in combination, that best serve as bases of support for stationary balances. Attempt to hold each balance still for three to five seconds. *Some students may need prompts.*
Dynamic balance requires body management when the body is moving	Explore different ways to travel in general space without losing balance (falling). Add starting and stopping to this dynamic balance.
	Pretend you are walking on a tightrope keeping one foot in front of the other starting and stopping as you choose.
	Travel on different body parts with body control, starting and stopping as you choose.
The most common weight transference is feet to feet in locomotor actions. Weight transference can be from feet to feet, feet to other body parts, and body part to body part exclusive of feet.	Gallop and skip in general space transferring weight momentarily from one foot to the other, maintaining balance while starting, stopping, and moving.
	Explore traveling and transferring weight with feet and other body parts in combination.
	Explore traveling and transferring weight on body parts other than feet.
	🚧 ***Do not allow traveling on hands alone.***
	Transfer weight from your feet to rounded back while at a low level, creating a rocking motion. *Some children will be ready for the transfer from feet to rounded back with a return to the feet and a standing position.*
	Transfer weight from one side to the other side using a stretched body at a low level, creating a side roll.
	Explore transferring weight from body part to body part within your personal space—without moving throughout the room.
	Balance on your chosen base of support; transfer your weight to another body part or body parts to balance on a new base of support.

Making the Connection: In a round-off, the hands and feet alternate taking on the role of supporting the body in a step-like weight transfer.

a

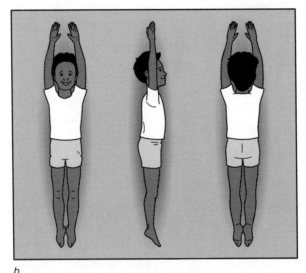

b

FIGURE 4.5 Transfer of weight (*a*) feet to back and (*b*) side to side.

Rocking in a curled body shape.

ACTIONS

Actions of the body include travel (locomotors), elevation (jumping, landing), and turning. Although some of these actions occur naturally in play, all children need guidance in the correct execution of the actions and their application for specific skills and for safety. Locomotors, jumping, and landing are skills typically taught early in elementary physical education. Learning experiences and critical elements of the skills can be found in many quality physical education textbooks and websites.

In the learning experiences in chapters 5 through 7 you will see that travel (locomotors), jumping and landing, and turning are corequisite skills used in many of the learning experiences. Therefore, a quality foundation of skill development is imperative to extend the educational gymnastics experience.

Cognitive	Performance
Locomotor actions on the feet include walking, running, galloping, skipping, hopping, jumping, leaping, and sliding sideways. All are used in educational gymnastics.	Walk in general space with body management (no crashes, no collisions with others, always looking for open space). Repeat with galloping, skipping, hopping (on one foot), and sliding sideways.
Traveling on different body parts involves transfer of weight from one body part to another.	Explore ways to travel on body parts other than your feet and on body parts in combination with your feet. Remember to be aware of others and use balanced stops. *This exploration of locomotors by children often results in crawling, creeping, rolling sideways, as well as a variety of ways to use hands and feet.* ▲ ***Traveling only on hands should not be permitted.***
Proper execution for the airborne actions as well as balanced landings must be in the repertoire of skills for all children.	Jump forward from two feet to two feet, landing in a balanced position.
	Jump upward from two feet to two feet, landing in a balanced position.
	Approach an imaginary line on the floor with two or three running steps, take off on one foot and land on two feet in a balanced position—no wiggles, no wobbles, no falling down.
	Practice jumping for height to increase elevation and create increased time in the air.
	Try making shapes with body parts and the total body while airborne. Focus on balanced landings.
Taking off on one foot and landing on the other foot is called leaping. It is the last of the locomotor skills to be mastered by children and is typically combined with running. Landing safely on one foot is an advanced airborne and balance combination.	Run or jog in open space. Leap by taking off on one foot, momentarily land on the other foot, and continue your travel, remembering body management in flight and in landing.
	Practice leaping for increased distance and increased height, always with balanced landings.
Turning while airborne is often a favorite action, and one that children can easily master. The turn is around the vertical axis, and the landing should be on two feet or on one foot quickly followed by the other.	Explore jumping and turning a quarter turn to your right. Use the twisting motion as you become airborne. Repeat to your left.
	Explore half and three-quarter turns both left and right.
	▲ ***Safely landing on the feet in the previous learning experiences demonstrates the option for individual children to be prompted to try the full turn.***

Making the Connection: Travel, jumping, landing, and turns will all be added to balance and weight transfer learning experiences as children create gymnastics sequences and routines (figures 4.6, 4.7, and 4.8). They will also be used when exploring the mount, travel, and dismount on gymnastics equipment. Jumping and landing are the introductory and concluding skills for much of gymnastics.

Travel on two hands and two feet.

Photo courtesy of the authors.

FIGURE 4.6 Travel on body parts other than two feet.

FIGURE 4.7   Jumping and landing for height (two feet to two feet).

FIGURE 4.8   Jump turn (half turn).

BODY SHAPES

The total body and body parts create the shapes: round, narrow, wide, and twisted. The shapes can also be symmetrical or asymmetrical. Unlike the actions discussed earlier, these actions require the child to hold the shapes like a statue.

Cognitive	Performance
Rounded shapes are created by curling the spine.	Standing on two feet, curl the spine forward, creating a rounded body shape.
	Explore rounded shapes on different bases of support.
Narrow shapes are created by the closeness of body parts.	Standing on two feet, create a narrow body shape with all free body parts close to the body; repeat with the arms stretched high above the head; repeat on one foot.
	Explore narrow body shapes on different bases of support.
Wide shapes are created by extending body parts away from the body.	Standing on two feet, extend free body parts away from the body to create a wide shape; repeat on one foot.
	Explore wide body shapes on different bases of support by extending free body parts away from the base of support.
Twisted body shapes are created by twisting the trunk and body parts (alone or together) while the base of support remains still. *Crossing the arms or legs, a common response of children, does not result in a twisted shape.*	Standing on two feet, twist the trunk, keeping the feet stationary, to create a twisted shape; repeat on one foot. Explore twisted body shapes on different bases of support.
Symmetrical shapes are formed when the two sides of the body are identical. Asymmetrical, or nonsymmetrical (*a term easier for children to understand*) shapes are formed when the two sides of the body are not identical.	Stand on two feet with the arms in identical positions—stretched forward, backward, high in the air, bent. This shape is symmetrical.
	Stand on one foot with the arms positioned as described above. This shape is nonsymmetrical. Why?
	Explore symmetrical and nonsymmetrical shapes on different bases of support.

Making the Connection: Body shapes are critical to the success of many weight transfer actions, that is, wide for a cartwheel, narrow for a log roll, and curled for a safety or shoulder roll. Body shapes can be added to the various jumping and landing experiences on the floor as well as on and off gymnastics equipment (figure 4.9). Symmetrical and asymmetrical shapes add challenges to the airborne phase of jumping and landing. These shapes will be combined with balancing and weight transfer in chapters 5 through 7. For example, one challenge may be to balance symmetrically and then use an asymmetrical shape to move out of the balance. Children will also be asked to explore symmetry while inverted.

FIGURE 4.9   Jumping and making shapes in the air.

SPACE AWARENESS

Where the body is moving is the focus of space awareness. The concepts of space awareness add depth and variety to children's movement vocabulary and skill responses.

Concepts

- Personal (self) and general space
- Directions
  - Forward, backward, up, down, right, left, clockwise, counterclockwise
- Levels
  - High, medium, low
- Pathways: On the floor, in the air
  - Straight, curved, zigzag
- Extensions
  - Far, near, large, small

PERSONAL AND GENERAL SPACE

All movement takes place in either personal or general space.

The awareness of personal space and the space of others is critical for safety in all movement.

Cognitive	Performance
Personal space is space surrounding the student when they are stationary, including the space for stretching, curling, and twisting. It is also the student's space when they are moving.	Explore the space surrounding the body when standing, sitting, and lying down. Stretch the total body; stretch free body parts. Curl the spine; bend free body parts. Twist the trunk; twist free body parts.
General space is the total shared space of the physical education work area within the boundaries established by the teacher.	Walk, hop, gallop, and skip in general space, stopping on signal without losing balance.
	Remember that your personal space travels with you.
	Run or jog in general space, always with an awareness of others and their personal space.
	Leap and jump in general space. *The practice of leaping and jumping will be in the general space designed by the teacher and is usually combined with a run. Add height and turns to jumping as appropriate.*
	Travel in general space using various body parts.
	Do not allow traveling on hands alone.

Making the Connection: All gymnastics learning experiences take place in either personal or general space, and in combinations of personal and general space.

DIRECTIONS

Directions for total body and individual body part movement are forward, backward, right, left, up, down, clockwise turning, and counterclockwise turning.

Cognitive	Performance
Directions can be explored with various body parts.	Standing in personal space, explore movements you can do with your arms in a forward direction: push, pull, various pathways. Explore movements with your arms: backward, sideways, up, down, clockwise circles, and counterclockwise circles.
	On your back, explore directional movement with your legs.
	Combine arm and leg directions.
	Move your legs to the side while your arms come forward. Explore other ways you can contrast directions.
Travel for children in general space should begin in a forward direction for awareness of others and safety. *Children often think of forward as the front of the room, but forward direction is the way that the child is facing when stationary and when moving.*	Travel throughout general space in a forward direction with your favorite locomotor, stopping on signal in a balanced position.
	Travel with a variety of locomotors, changing the locomotor (e.g., hop, then gallop) each time you hear the signal or meet another person. Always remember body management.
With sufficient space for safety, children can move backward, side to side, and with clockwise and counterclockwise pivots and spins.	Walk backward, traveling with control and stopping in a balanced position. Always look over your shoulder when traveling backward.
	Try galloping, hopping, or skipping backward.
	♦ ***Running is not a safe option for backward travel.***
	Travel side to side with a sliding step, stop, pivot, and continue your side-to-side travel.
	Travel side to side with a sliding step, stop, and turn or spin clockwise or counterclockwise, always with awareness of others and their space. Continue your side-to-side travel.
The direction of up and down can be performed in personal space, with travel and with turns.	In personal space, move the arms up and down, move them alternately up and down. Move the total body up and down.
	Travel forward, stop, lower your body to a medium level, pivot with a half turn, jump up, and continue to travel. Repeat.
	Travel forward, jump up and do a quarter turn, and continue traveling. When comfortable, try a half turn. Repeat.

Making the Connection: In gymnastics children explore directions and changes of directions with the total body and with body parts in general space and in personal space on the ground, floor, or individual mats. When children are ready, these directional concepts are introduced on low beams and benches.

LEVELS

All balances and all movement of total body and body parts take place at either high, medium, or low level. Levels are explored by placing as much of the body as possible in one location (figure 4.10).

Cognitive	Performance
High level is the area above the shoulders. Medium level is the area of space between the shoulders and the knees. Low level is the area below the knees.	Stand on two feet and extend your arms to the highest level you can reach. Add a jump.
	Lying on the floor, curl your body into a round shape at low level. Explore other body shapes you can make at low level.
	In between high and low is medium level. Explore body shapes when most of your body is at medium level.
	Try symmetrical and nonsymmetrical shapes at each of the levels.
	Walk throughout general space, stretching the body and extending the arms to their highest level. Add jumping and leaping to increase your height.
	Slide sideways at medium level.
	Crawl, creep, or slither at low level.
	Explore different ways to travel at each level, changing levels on the teacher's signal. Remember that you can travel on body parts other than your feet.

Making the Connection: Various gymnastic balances, weight transfer, and travel experiences can be created using any or all three levels. For example, a child's creation of a simple balance, roll, balance sequence may be a balance on the stomach, followed by a log roll, and ending in a balance on two hands and two feet all at a low level. Children will later be challenged to add a change of levels to their sequence.

FIGURE 4.10 High, medium, and low levels.

PATHWAYS

Movement pathways include straight, curved, and zigzag. Those pathways may be on the floor or in the air. They can be made with body parts or with the total body as the child travels.

Cognitive	Performance
Pathways on the floor are created as children travel, as if footprints are being left on the surface.	Travel in a straight pathway, stop, pause, or make a sharp quarter turn when you meet another person or a boundary of the work area. Remember to move with no curves or zigzags, only straight lines.
	Travel with your favorite locomotor in a straight pathway; you may need to travel backward or side to side as well as forward to maintain straight pathways.
	Travel in curved pathways throughout general space. Remember that you make the pathway with footprints on the floor, not by waving your arms.
	Travel in zigzag pathways—zig and zag, side to side as you travel forward.
	Try a zigzag pathway as you travel backward. *Children named this the "zagzig."*
Traveling straight, curved, and zigzag pathways can be explored using different body parts.	Explore different ways to travel in each pathway. Remember that you can travel on body parts other than your feet.
Straight, curved, and zigzag pathways can also be performed in the air. Aerial pathways with wands, hoops, and streamers are the content of artistic gymnastics. Children enjoy exploring these pathways with scarves and streamers.	Lie on your back and use your legs and arms to explore straight, curved, and zigzag aerial pathways with your arms.
	Travel in general space and explore aerial pathways with a scarf or streamer.
	▲ ***Remind students of being aware of others as they travel with scarves and streamers.***

Making the Connection: Pathway approaches to gymnastics equipment and apparatus are often included to enhance a routine or to work in crowded spaces around other children. Exploration and travel on benches and beams, by necessity, will be in a straight pathway.

EXTENSIONS

Extensions represent the awareness of the amount of space occupied by body parts or the total body when stationary or moving. This awareness is an important component of safety when occupying or moving in personal space, when sharing space with others in general space, and when using equipment. Extensions of body parts can be described as near or far in their relation to the body (figure 4.11). Body movements are described as large or small.

Cognitive	Performance
Large movements and far extensions occupy more space and occur away from the center of the body. Small body movements and near extensions of body parts occur close to the center of the body.	Standing in your self-space, extend the arms upward, backward, or to the sides, without interfering in the space of others. Extend them far from the body. Repeat and keep them close to the body.
	On different bases of support, explore extensions of free body parts, keeping them close to the body. Extend them as far as possible from the body.
	Walk in general space using your regular steps; repeat with baby steps and then with giant steps.
	Hop on one foot, keeping the arms close to your body making small movements; run and leap, extending your arms away from your body making large movements.
	Explore other movements to contrast small and large.

Making the Connection: Near and far extensions of body parts change the shape of balances in gymnastics as well as the travel in sequences. Body management for efficiency and safety may be controlled by a simple adjustment of extensions. For example, walking on a beam requires arm extension away from the body to aid balance. When walking on the floor the arms are close to the body.

FIGURE 4.11   Extensions near and far in relation to the body: *(top)* hands near and far from each other; *(bottom)* body parts close and body parts far.

EFFORT

The idea of how the body moves is addressed in the effort concepts. The four dimensions of time, weight (force), space, and flow are taught by emphasizing two extremes. With experience, children learn that a spectrum of movement can occur within each extreme.

Concepts

- Time
  - Sudden, sustained
- Weight (force)
  - Heavy, light
- Space
  - Direct, flexible
- Flow
  - Bound, free

TIME

The movement of the total body and of body parts can be described as sudden or sustained and fast or slow, with varying degrees of each. Some movements may require acceleration, whereas others need deceleration.

Cognitive	Performance
Body parts can move slowly or quickly.	Extend your hands far apart from each other. Slowly bring them together. When they almost touch, quickly take them back out. Repeat, bringing your hands in quickly and extending them out slowly.
The body can move slowly or quickly from one body shape to the next.	Create a wide body shape. Slowly change the shape to narrow.
	Create a wide body shape on two feet. Quickly bring your feet together, making a narrow shape on two feet.
	Explore other body shapes with quick transitions and then with slow transitions.
	🚧 *Always remember body control for safety.*
The body can move slowly or quickly from one movement to the next.	Travel quickly in general space. On the signal, transition to slow travel. Travel at medium speed (somewhere between fast and slow). Explore different ways to travel, contrasting fast, medium, and slow speeds.
	Explore continual travel, accelerating and decelerating when you choose.

Making the Connection: In gymnastics, the movement into and out of balances is slow. Weight transfers may be slow, fast, or medium speed. A back walkover is slow, a handspring fast, and a cartwheel is at medium speed.

WEIGHT (FORCE)

Weight (force) in movement is categorized as heavy or light. Both require controlled muscular tension.

Cognitive	Performance
The focus of weight (force) as an effort component is on movement, not on a shape. *Young children often equate heavy weight (force) as a body shape or balance that shows muscles and power.*	Walk in general space with heavy force, stomping your feet. Travel lightly in general space as if sneaking up on someone.
	Explore other ways of travel and notice how you must use your muscles differently to contrast heavy and light movements.
	Remember to travel on body parts other than just your feet.

Making the Connection: Force will be used for travel in sequences and movement on equipment and apparatus. Body management for force requires an understanding of how to use muscular tension for control and safety. You will see differences in force in a gymnastics floor routine.

SPACE

Space, as an effort component, refers to the use of space—direct or flexible. Direct paths use less space than flexible ones.

Cognitive	Performance
Movements may necessitate direct paths or flexible paths.	Locate a space in the gym and travel a direct path to it. Take the same path back to where you started.
	Travel to the same spot but make your path as indirect as possible. Use as much of the general space as possible before reaching your destination.

Making the Connection: Approaches to equipment and apparatus for mounts as well as the path for the approach for jumping for height require direct paths. Flexible paths are incorporated into sequences and travel on apparatus and are often controlled by space, location, and others.

FLOW

The flow of a movement refers to the continuity and may be bound (stoppable at any point) or free (unstoppable from beginning to end).

Cognitive	Performance
Some movements are bound and can be stopped at any time, whereas others are continuous.	With your hands and feet as bases of support, extend one leg as far as you can and stop. Repeat and stop when almost straight. Now, extend all the way. These bound movements can be stopped, with control, at any time.
	In your personal space, jump high in the air. Stop in a balanced landing. Can you jump and stop in midair? Why not? Gravity! This free-flow movement is continuous from takeoff to flight to landing.

Making the Connection: The effort component of flow affects the study of weight transference. Some transfers (jumping and landing, all in-flight actions, rolling) are free flow for safe completion of the action. Transfers into and out of balances are stoppable. A functional understanding of flow is important for safety and for continuity in all gymnastics sequences and routines.

RELATIONSHIPS

The focus on interactions among the various components of a child's movement environment is relationships. Relationships may be between body parts, with manipulative equipment (i.e., balls, rackets, hockey sticks), with nonmanipulative equipment (i.e., benches, boxes, beams, ladders), or with others. Children work alone within the class, with partners, or within small groups. A partner may be of equal or unequal skill and size.

Concepts

- Between body parts
- With objects—manipulative, nonmanipulative
- With people

BETWEEN BODY PARTS

Locomotor, manipulative, and nonmanipulative movements all require an understanding of how one body part interacts with or is positioned in relation to other body parts to reach a specific outcome.

Cognitive	Performance
Body parts can be positioned in several ways in relation to other body parts—above, apart, together, in front of, beside, between, behind, over, under, below, around.	Slide sideways in general space, moving the lead foot just before the feet would touch. The relationship is beside. The feet never cross.
	Repeat with a gallop forward. The relationship is now in front and behind. Again, the feet never cross.
	Using two hands and two feet for a base of support, place your hands shoulder width apart and your feet together. The relationship is beside with hands apart and feet together (figure 4.12).
	Explore other positions in which you can place body parts in relation to other body parts.

Making the Connection: Good balance requires a stable base of support and body alignment. The relationship between body parts helps create stability and alignment. A tripod, for example, requires a triangle shape created by the relationship of hands and head for the base with the knees resting on the elbows for body alignment. The relationship between body parts is also important on equipment. When a child travels on the playground equipment or does a flip on the playground bars, the relationship of hands to the trunk is critical for success (figure 4.13).

FIGURE 4.12 Relationship of hands apart and feet together.

FIGURE 4.13 Relationships of body parts to equipment.

WITH OBJECTS

Relationships with objects are part of manipulative and nonmanipulative activities in physical education. Exclusive of rhythmical gymnastics, only the nonmanipulative relationship of student to equipment is developed in gymnastics.

Cognitive	Performance
Relationships with nonmanipulative equipment include exploration of equipment as well as directional travel in relation to equipment.	*Create an obstacle course for students to travel through.*
	Travel the obstacle course making safe choices to go under, over, around, and through.
	Travel safely onto, on, and off benches, step boxes, and large equipment at low levels.

Making the Connection: Balances and transference of weight may include learning experiences on low equipment in the gymnasium, on playground equipment, and on apparatus.

WITH PEOPLE

Relationships with people are part of every aspect of movement in physical education, whether simply being aware of others or working with others.

Cognitive	Performance
Relationships with people include working safely as an individual while all classmates are active, working with a partner, and working in a small group. All involve elements of safety and respect of the movement of others.	Travel through general space using your favorite locomotor, looking for open spaces. Increase or decrease your speed to avoid others and their space. Travel with a different locomotor each time you hear the signal. Remember that others are also traveling with different locomotors and speeds.
	With a partner, face each other and take turns being in the lead role as your partner matches the body shape that you create and your choice of locomotor.
	In a group of three, create wide shapes. Each person is at a different level (high, medium, and low).
	In a group of four, travel in general space in a follow-the-leader relationship. The leader changes on the signal. As a leader, you choose the locomotor, level, pathway, direction, force, and speed of travel.

Making the Connection: Partner gymnastics experiences include sharing balances, supporting balances, sequences for matching, and leading and following (balances, weight transfers, and travel).

Summary

The Movement Analysis Framework contains the skills and concepts of all games, all sports, gymnastics, and dance. It contains all the skills and movement concepts of educational gymnastics, and as such is the curricular content of gymnastics for children. A functional understanding, both cognitive and performance, of the Movement Analysis Framework is essential for children's work in gymnastics. A functional understanding of the framework provides the foundation for the learning experiences that, coupled with a child-centered approach to teaching, allows for individual differences in skill levels and a progression toward each child's potential in gymnastics. The experiences in this chapter will not only enrich the variety of ideas that children bring to an educational gymnastics learning experience but also generate more skilled responses. With learning experiences based on the Movement Analysis Framework instead of predetermined traditional gymnastics skills, all children enjoy and benefit from the gymnastics experiences.

References

Graham, G., Holt/Hale, S., Parker, M., Hall, T., and Patton, K. 2020. *Children Moving: A Reflective Approach to Teaching Physical Education*, 10th ed. New York: McGraw-Hill.

Holt/Hale, S., and Hall, T. 2016. *Lesson Planning for Elementary Physical Education: Meeting the National Standards and Grade-Level Outcomes*. Champaign, IL: Human Kinetics.

Stanley, S. 1969. *Physical Education: A Movement Orientation*. Montreal, Canada: McGraw-Hill.

Appendix A

SHAPES

Grades K, 1

Standard 2: The physically literate individual applies knowledge of concepts, principles, strategies, and tactics related to movement and performance.

Grade-Level Outcome

Forms wide, narrow, curled, and twisted body shapes (S1.E7.Kb)

Lesson Objectives

The learner will:

- Identify the basic shapes of wide, narrow, curled, and twisted
- Make the shapes with the body and body parts

Introduction

In the classroom, your teacher talks about the shapes of circles, squares, and triangles in mathematics. Your mom and dad talk about getting in shape for fitness. Our lesson today is about shapes in physical education, shapes that the body makes. There are four shapes: wide, narrow, curled, and twisted.

Grade 1: Relate to dance, gymnastics, and sports for children.

Learning Experience: Narrow Shapes

In self-space, students make narrow shapes, long and thin, stretching to be really narrow.

Cue: *Legs and arms close to the body or close together*

- Narrow shapes with the body in various positions: sitting, lying on the floor, standing
- Narrow shapes at different levels: low, medium, high (imagery: like a piece of spaghetti)

Learning Experience: Wide Shapes

In self-space, students make wide shapes by extending their arms and legs far to the sides.

Cue: *Legs and arms extended away from the body*

- Wide shapes with the body in various positions
- Wide shapes at different levels (imagery: like an open umbrella or a really big yawn)

Learning Experience: Curled Shapes

In self-space, students make curled or round shapes by curling the spine forward.

Cue: *Curling the spine*

- Curled shapes with the body in various positions
- Curled shapes at different levels (imagery: like a ball or the letter C)

Learning Experience: Twisted Shapes

In self-space, students make twisted shapes by rotating a body part around a stationary axis (model the twisting action as opposed to crossing legs and arms).

Cue: *Rotating the arms, legs, and trunk*

- Twisting of arms inward, outward
- Twisting the legs inward, outward
- Twisting the trunk clockwise, counterclockwise (imagery: like a pretzel or a shoestring in a knot)
- How many body parts can you twist?

Learning Experience: Combining Shapes and Actions: Transformers

We are going to combine body shapes and actions in an activity called Transformers. The word *transform* means to change from one thing to another—thus the name of the activity. You are going to be a transformer that changes shape four times. Your shapes will be wide, narrow, curled, and twisted. I will give the signal for changing shapes.

- Have the students make a wide shape in self-space—standing, sitting, or lying on the floor.
- Provide an eight-count signal for slowly changing from the wide shape to a narrow shape.
- Have students continue the shape and action sequence for all four shapes, emphasizing the slowness of the change and clear distinction of the shapes.

Grade 1

Students choose the order of the shapes.

Just for fun, have students name the transformer they created.

Learning Experience: Shape Statues

Divide the students into groups of four. Each person in the group makes one of the shapes. Students in each group touch to form a group statue that demonstrates each of the shapes. Connect the shapes to form a single statue by having each person touching one other person in the group.

Grade 2

Challenge students to travel in their group statue while maintaining shapes and connections.

Assessment

Have students respond by creating the body shape you name. You can also assess cognitive understanding by students' spoken responses to these questions:

- What body parts create narrow shapes?
- Wide shapes?
- Curled shapes?
- What is the key to creating a twisted shape?

Closure

- We had fun today being transformers and shape statues, but what were we studying? What was the objective of our lesson?
- What are the four body shapes?

Show the children pictures of the various body shapes in sports or physical activity contexts. (Watch for photos of local athletes in the newspaper.) Have the children identify the body shape shown in the action photo.

Grade 1

- Which of the shapes does a basketball player use in a defensive guarding position?
- Which shape does the gymnast use for forward and backward rolls?

Reflection

- Can the children use their whole bodies and body parts to make each of the shapes?
- Can they identify each of the shapes when demonstrated or when seen in photos of athletes in sports, gymnastics, or dance?

Reprinted by permission from S. Holt/Hale and T. Hall, *Lesson Planning for Elementary Physical Education: Meeting the National Standards and Grade-Level Outcomes*, (Champaign, IL: Human Kinetics, 2016), 61-62.

Appendix B

JUMPING AND LANDING

Grades 1, 2

Standard 1: The physically literate individual demonstrates competency in a variety of motor skills and movement patterns.

Grade-Level Outcomes

- Demonstrates two of the five critical elements for jumping and landing in a vertical plane (S1.E4.1)
- Demonstrates four of the five critical elements for jumping and landing in a vertical plane (S1.E4.2)

Lesson Objectives

The learner will:

- Bend the knees and swing the arms in preparation for jumping
- Swing arms upward when jumping
- Land in a balanced position with bent hips, knees, and ankles

Critical Elements for Jumping and Landing (Vertical Plane)

- Hips, knees, and ankles bend in preparation for jumping action.
- Arms extend upward as body propels upward.
- Body extends and stretches upward while in flight.
- Hips, knees, and ankles bend on landing.
- Shoulders, knees, and ankles align for balance after landing.

Materials and Equipment

- Large mat, milk crate (box filled with large empty cans from cafeteria or packed with newspaper), or 12-inch (30 cm) platform structure
- Stretch rope with balloons suspended
- Colored 1-inch (2.5 cm) tape
- Masking tape

Introduction

During our last lesson on jumping, you practiced jumping for distance. You learned that the arms swing back and forth and the knees bend in preparation for jumping. We also talked about the importance of bending the knees when landing to absorb the force. Today, you are going to jump for height. Your arms still swing back and forth in preparation; the knees still need to bend when landing. So, what is different about jumping for height? The arms now swing upward as you jump high in the air, and you now land in your same space. Ask your neighbor, "What is the same when jumping for distance and when jumping for height? What is different?"

Learning Experience: Review of Jumping Action

Safety check: Check for sufficient space for jumping forward.

With students scattered in general space, allow several minutes of jumping forward with practice review of the swing and spring action of the arms and legs. Students should bend the hips, knees, and ankles for soft landings.

Assessment

Initiate peer assessment of critical elements of arms, legs, and landings. Students should try to achieve a score of 3 for all three critical elements. The student does three jumps, and the peer focuses on one at a time—preparation, body airborne, and landing.

Learning Experience: Vertical Jumping

- Students jump for height in self-space with swing and spring, coupled with soft landings.
- Arms extend upward for height.
- Challenge the students to jump really high by stretching the body upward and reaching toward the ceiling or sky. Imagery: jumping high to receive a ball in basketball, football, or baseball.

Note: Emphasize the need for soft landings as the height of the jump increases. A soft landing is crucial when jumping for height; the student is looking upward.

- Continue practice of vertical jumping for several minutes, observing the class as a whole and individual students for critical elements (extension upward, soft landings with knees bent) and providing individual assistance as needed.

Learning Experience: Stations for Practice

Jumping for height, jumping for maximum distance, and jumping personal height

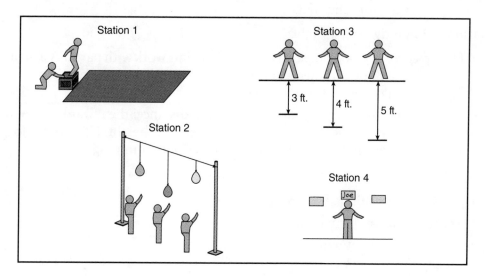

Jumping for Height

Station 1: Jumping Off a Crate or Box

- The focus is on jumping upward, not forward.
- The temptation is just to step off the crate. Jump high in the air as you take off from the crate. Don't jump for distance. Focus on a good landing by bending the knees to absorb the force.
- Stand beside the crate with one hand extended at a height that will challenge students to extend really high on the jump; adjust the hand placement to provide a challenge to each student.

Safety check: Students may not jump off the crate unless another student is holding the crate to prevent slipping.

Station 2: Jumping to Tap a Balloon

- Suspend balloons at various heights. Students jump to tap the balloon of their choice. The focus is on two-foot takeoffs and two-foot landings.
- Balloons suspended in this manner have a built-in increased challenge. As the student taps the balloon, the string holding it wraps around the rope, raising the balloon. Each successful jump creates a higher target.
- The stretch rope can also be angled higher or lower by adjusting one end of the rope where it is attached to the pole, enabling individual challenge to the student.

Station 3: Jumping for Distance

- Standing behind the starting line, students jump for distance—3 feet, 4 feet, 5 feet (90, 120, 150 cm).
- The focus is on balanced landings.

Safety check: Always position students with their backs to the wall so that they are jumping away from the wall.

Station 4: Jumping Your Height

- Place pieces of masking tape on the wall. Students work with partners. Partner A lies on the floor with heels at the starting line; partner B places a piece of tape on the floor just above partner A's head.
- The challenge is to jump your own height in distance; the reward is to write your name on the piece of tape that indicates your height. ("Jump Jim Joe," a folk dance, is an excellent revisitation practice for jumping.)

Assessment

- Teacher observation at station 1
- Peer assessment during lesson
- Formal assessment of mature pattern in grade 3

Closure

- What was the focus of our lesson today? What kind of jump did you perform? (Stand with your feet together, legs straight, arms at sides. Model as you ask the following questions and as students give their responses.)

- Am I ready to jump? What do I need to do with my arms? My knees? What will I need to remember when I land?

- What is different with my arms when I jump for height as compared with when I jump for distance?

- Is jumping upward needed in gymnastics, dance, or games and sports? How? Why?

Reflection

- Do students swing their arms back and forth in preparation for the jump and then upward for height as they jump?

- Do they land with knees bent to absorb the force?

- Do the students achieve vertical projection, not horizontal, on the vertical jump?

- Do they achieve horizontal airborne time, not vertical, on the jump for distance?

Reprinted by permission from S. Holt/Hale and T. Hall, *Lesson Planning for Elementary Physical Education: Meeting the National Standards and Grade-Level Outcomes*, (Champaign, IL: Human Kinetics, 2016), 92-94.

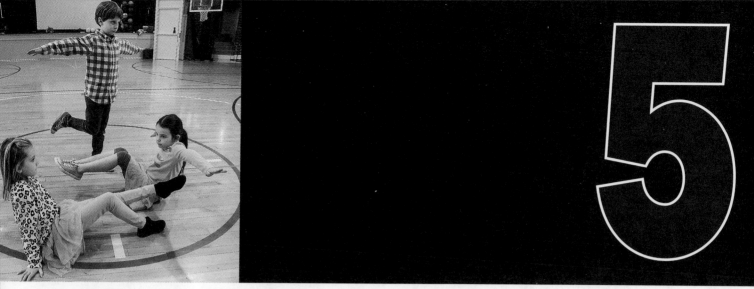

Photo courtesy of the authors.

The Foundational Skills of Balance

In gymnastics, balance is described as the body maintained in a still position. The ability to maintain balance and regain balance is one element of body control. The skill of balance leads to confidence and increases opportunities for physical activity and enhances the quality of all stages of life. This chapter provides foundational balance learning experiences for the body awareness and body control essential for good balance. The focus begins with learning and applying the principles of balance and progresses to balancing in shapes and levels as aligned with the Movement Analysis Framework covered in chapter 4.

Mini Index for Learning Experiences

Balance Concepts 65
   Stillness 65
      Introduction to Stillness 66
   Bases of Support and Stability 66
      Exploring Bases of Support and Clarifying a Good Gymnastic Balance 67
      Muscular Tension 69
      Weight Distribution 70
      Number of Bases of Support 71
      Travel, Stop, Balance 72
   Alignment, Extensions, and Counterbalance 72
      Alignment 73
      Alignment With Extension of Free Body Parts 74
      Counterbalance Extensions 75
      Partner Counterbalance Using Counter-Resistance 76
      Partner Counterbalance Using Counter-Tension 77
Balancing Using Body Shapes and Levels 78
   Balancing Shapes and Levels 78
      Wide, Narrow, Curled, and Twisted Shapes 79
      Symmetrical and Nonsymmetrical Shapes 81
      Combining Shapes and Symmetry 82
      Balancing at Different Levels 82
      Combining Shapes and Levels 84

BALANCE CONCEPTS

A functional understanding (cognitive and performance) of several balance concepts is critical for children's work. Gymnastic balance requires a degree of challenge that will cause children to become unstable or off-balance if they do not follow balance concepts. In the following list, in parentheses next to the description of the concepts, is the grade level at which most students are cognitively ready for the concept to be introduced. The grade-level decisions are based on child development research and the authors' years of experience teaching children. It is important to emphasize the concepts in all grades, especially as the balances become more complex.

- *Stillness* aids children in the "feel" of a good balance. After they attain a balance, absolutely no movement should occur for three to five seconds (kindergarten).
- *The base of support* is defined as the body part or parts in contact with the floor that support the body (kindergarten).
- *Resting positions are not gymnastic balances.* This concept clarifies what is considered a gymnastic balance. Children often confuse a resting position as an option for a gymnastic balance. A child may say they are balancing on their seat and legs when they are sitting or balancing on two feet when standing. Although they have a base of support, these are not gymnastic balances. A gymnastic balance brings on a challenge that a resting position does not (kindergarten).
- *Muscular tension helps to maintain a balance.* Muscular tension, or tightening the muscles, in the body parts that serve as the base of support helps to maintain the balance. Tightening the core or midsection muscles is also important (grade 1).
- *Weight distribution* should be evenly established over the stronger supporting body parts (grade 1).
- *Body alignment* over the base of support and in relation to extended body parts aids in maintaining balance (grade 2).
- *The extension of free body parts*, those not serving as the base of support, helps body alignment (grade 2).
- *Counterbalance* using extended free body parts in opposition results in a more stable balance. Counterbalance is especially useful in more complex balances (grade 2).
- *A wide base of support* is more stable than a narrow base of support (grade 2).

In the learning experiences that follow, students apply the preceding balance concepts to the exploration of the bases of support. Locomotors and a functional understanding of the movement concepts (chapter 4) are prerequisite skills for these tasks.

Stillness

Cognitive: Stillness is needed to maintain a balance.

Skills: To maintain stillness.

Criteria: Three to five seconds.

Safety: Personal space.

Equipment and organization: No equipment; students in personal space.

INTRODUCTION TO STILLNESS

Learning experiences	Teaching tips
In your personal space, balance on one foot, holding as still as you can. Balance on the other foot, holding absolutely still.	*Emphasize stillness for the balance.*
Find a partner and stand back to back. Take two giant steps apart and face each other. Balance on one foot. Your partner will count one hippopotamus, two hippopotamus, three . . . rest. Were you able to stay absolutely still for the three seconds? Now your partner will balance on one foot as you count. Repeat the balance, trying for five seconds of stillness.	
Repeat the balance on the other foot. Remember, no wiggles, no wobbles.	*Emphasize stillness for three to five seconds. Demonstrate a good balance on one foot and contrast with one that is wobbly.*
Challenge: Facing your partner, balance on your chosen foot, seeing who can balance the longest without moving. Repeat with the other foot.	*Remind students that stillness is total body stillness, not just loss of balance with the other foot touching the floor.*

Students explore bases of support.
Photo courtesy of the authors.

Bases of Support and Stability

Cognitive: Base of support is the body part or parts in contact with the floor and supporting the body. A gymnastic balance brings on a challenge that is different from a resting position. Muscular tension and weight distribution aid in stability.

Skills: To maintain stillness on various bases of support using muscular tension and weight distribution for stability.

Criteria: Demonstrate a variety of balances (defined by the base of support) using tight muscles and weight distribution to maintain stillness for three to five seconds.

Safety: Personal space. Ensure that mats (if used) do not slide. Allow recovery time because focusing on muscular tension may tire students.

Equipment and organization: No equipment or individual small mats; students in personal space.

EXPLORING BASES OF SUPPORT AND CLARIFYING A GOOD GYMNASTIC BALANCE

Learning experiences	Teaching tips
The base of support is the part or parts of your body that touch the floor and hold you in a balance.	*Use as an introduction to the learning experiences before sending students to personal space.*
• What was your base of support in the last balance? • What is my base of support now? • What is your base of support? • What is my base of support now? Our positions now are not gymnastic balances. To be a gymnastic balance, you must challenge yourself beyond typical daily body positions such as sitting, standing, and lying down.	• *Wait on response of "one foot."* • *Stand on two feet and face the students who are sitting. Wait on response of "two feet."* • *Wait on response of "seat and legs."* • *Demonstrate a balance on one foot and two hands. Wait on response.*
In your sitting position, grasp your knees with your arms and raise your feet just off the floor. Your base of support is now your seat only; this is a gymnastic balance. Today you are going to explore different body parts that can serve as bases of support for gymnastic balances.	*See figure 5.1.*
In personal space, see how many different body parts can serve as your base of support. You will combine body parts and remain still for three to five seconds. After three to five seconds, try a new one. If you cannot maintain stillness after a few attempts, explore another option. 🚧 **For safety reasons, do not include your head as a base of support and do not try to balance on just hands.**	*While students are exploring, walk around and make note of the different bases you observe. Share examples of bases of support you observed. List them on whiteboard or display on screen. Add additional ones that serve as good bases.*
Now, I will name the base of support, and you will create the balance. Focus on stillness for three to five seconds; no wiggles, no wobbles. Let's start with one foot.	
Look around; almost everyone looks the same. Create a balance on one foot that is different. Explore as many ways to balance on one foot as you can hold still for three to five seconds.	*Pinpoint what you see to encourage variety.* *See figure 5.2.*
Listed on the board (or screen) are bases of support I observed when I watched you work. Practice to see how many ways you can balance using the base of support I read from our list. After three to five seconds of stillness, try another way to balance on that base of support. • Two feet, two hands • Two feet, one hand • One foot, two hands • One foot, opposite hand • Two knees, two elbows, two feet • Two knees, two elbows • Two elbows, one knee, one foot • Two knees, one elbow • Seat and one hand • Seat only • Back only • Stomach only	*Use the examples provided and others that you observed.*

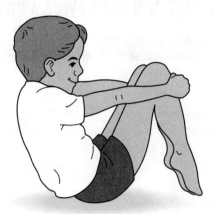

FIGURE 5.1   Balance on seat.

FIGURE 5.2   Demonstrating variety while balancing on one foot.

MUSCULAR TENSION

Learning experiences	Teaching tips
Some balances that you explored may have been more difficult than others to hold still. The secret to the stillness is muscular tension—tight muscles. Sitting in your own space, extend your legs on the floor. In this position, tighten all the muscles in your legs and hips. Make them feel as strong as you can. Keep the leg and hip muscles tight, extend your arms above your head, and tighten all the muscles in your shoulders and arms.	
Return to sitting with your legs crossed. Focus on tightening all the muscles in your body, keeping this same position. Remember to breathe.	
Standing in your personal space, tighten the legs first, your hips, and your tummy muscles. Extend your arms to a high level and tighten the shoulders and arms. Relax and shake it out!	*This is fun to do with pretend screwdrivers starting at the ankle, knees, and then hips.*
We are going to repeat some of the balances you did earlier, but this time with a focus on tight muscles. When I name the base of support, create the balance and hold it very still by concentrating on using tight muscles. Your muscles will be tight on the body parts supporting you and the ones that are free. For example, in the balance using one foot and two hands, one leg is free. I should see those strong muscles in your balance. You should look like a statue. • Two feet, one hand • One foot, two hands • One foot, opposite hand • Seat only • Back only • Stomach only	*Demonstrate and point out the free leg and tight muscles.* *Use the examples provided and others that you choose.*

Balance on two hands, two feet, and two knees.

Photo courtesy of the authors.

WEIGHT DISTRIBUTION

Learning experiences	Teaching tips
The next few balances include your head. For these balances you are going to use at least three other bases of support with the head.	*Use as an introduction to the learning experiences before sending students to personal space. Later, after learning the safety shoulder roll, most students will be ready for two additional bases of support with the head, and mats will be used.*
The secret is to have your weight distributed evenly on the strongest body parts that are your base of support, allowing your head, the weakest part, simply to touch.	*Demonstrate a balance on two hands and one foot, and then gently touch your head to the mat.*
In your personal space, balance on two knees and two hands. Gently touch your head to the floor. Keep your muscles tight.	
Explore other bases of support you can combine with your head. Remember, you must have at least three additional bases of support, to support your weight. If this hurts your head, you are placing too much weight on it. Remember, the head only touches the floor. The head should not be supporting your weight.	*See figure 5.3.*

FIGURE 5.3 Balances using the head and three or more additional bases of support.

NUMBER OF BASES OF SUPPORT

Learning experiences	Teaching tips
Balance in your personal space on four bases of support. Count and make sure you use four—no more, no less.	
Change your base of support but make sure that four body parts are touching the floor.	*See figure 5.4.*
When I say a number, show me a balance with that many body parts as your base of support. I will ask for two balances with each number.	*Continue to call random numbers 1 through 6.*

FIGURE 5.4   Example balances on four bases of support.

TRAVEL, STOP, BALANCE

Learning experiences	Teaching tips
Next, you are going to travel in general space. I will name a locomotor skill followed by a number. On the signal to stop, you will freeze in a balance that has a base of support that matches the number. While you are traveling, think about the balance you will create. Remember that when you travel in general space, you take your personal space with you. When you stop to balance, you will be in your personal space and can safely execute your balance. Try to be creative and don't forget the tight muscles for stillness.	Observe for good use of general space; students should never be close enough to touch as they travel. On signal, ensure they are in personal space before balancing. Use the examples provided and others that you choose. If mats are used, remind students to move around, not over, them.
• Walk backward, 4. • Gallop, 6. • Slide sideways in a zigzag pathway, 1. • Run at a safe speed, 3. • Hop in a straight pathway, 5. • Skip, 2. Choose your way to travel. On the signal, freeze in your favorite balance that you have created today.	
Challenge: Select three of your favorite balances from today. Each one must have a different base of support. Practice each, holding still for three to five seconds before practicing the next one.	Some students may need guidance in making selections.
Watch your partner perform one of their balances and give them a thumbs up if they were able to hold it still for three to five seconds. Now, your partner will watch you and assess your stillness. Continue taking turns. If you finish before the signal to stop, try the balances your partner did.	Groups of two: One active and one assessing, taking turns.

Alignment, Extensions, and Counterbalance

Cognitive: Body alignment over the base of support and extension of free body parts aid in balance. Extensions in opposite directions create a counterbalance that provides stability for more difficult balances. Partners can use counter-resistance and counter-tension, employing each other for counterbalance.

Skills: Balance on a variety of bases of support with body alignment including extensions of free body parts. Counterbalance by demonstrating extensions in opposing directions with several challenging balances both alone and using counter-resistance and counter-tension with a partner.

Criteria: Tight muscles within the extensions, body parts over the base of support aligned, and extensions used for counterbalance.

Safety: Personal space. If mats are used, ensure that they do not slide. If large mats are used, have students take turns rather than share space. Encourage slow movements for counterbalance learning experiences. Watch for fatigue and allow a muscle rest if needed.

Equipment and organization: None or individual small mats; larger shared mats for partner counterbalance challenges; students in personal space for individual tasks. Handouts for partner counterbalances (no pencils needed).

ALIGNMENT

Learning experiences	Teaching tips
You can now do several balances, many of which you may not have tried before. Using some of the same balances you have created, you are going to make them even better.	*Use as an introduction to the learning experiences before sending students to personal space.*
Stand up as if you are in the army standing at attention. Yes, you can act as if you are saluting if you wish. Tighten the muscles in your whole body, remembering not to hold your breath. Your body is in alignment. Now, stretch your arms high above your head, which is the ending position used in gymnastics. Let's call it the "Ta-da." Your arms should be aligned over your shoulders, the shoulders over your hips, and the hips over your feet. Sometimes this posture is hard to feel but easier to see.	*See figure 5.5.*
Find a partner nearby and check each other for alignment: arms over shoulders, shoulders over hips, hips over feet. Return to your personal space and show me the "Ta-da" one more time.	*Groups of two: One active and one assessing, taking turns.*

FIGURE 5.5   "Ta-da."

ALIGNMENT WITH EXTENSION OF FREE BODY PARTS

Learning experiences	Teaching tips
Balance on one foot. Extend arms over your head. Alignment and tight muscles are now super important to help you maintain your balance. For the next several balances, you are going to tighten your muscles, align your balance over your base of support, and extend free body parts away from your base of support.	*Use as an introduction to the learning experiences. Students can remain in personal space.*
Balance on two feet and one hand. Extend the other arm. Remember, tight muscles and no wiggles, no wobbles. The arm that is extended is called your free body part; it is not part of your base of support. Align your body over your base of support. Stretch the free arm for a full extension.	*Using a student for demonstration, pinpoint the stretch and the extension (see chapter 3, figure 3.3).*
Explore focusing on alignment and extension of free body parts while you try these balances: • Two hands, one foot • Two knees, two feet • Back or spine only • Stomach only • Seat only	*Students may need help in determining the free body parts. Teacher or student demonstrations with naming the free body parts will be helpful.*
Challenge: Balance on the back of your shoulders, back of head, upper arms. Place your hands on your hips and extend your legs as high as you can in the air. Tighten the muscles in your stomach and legs as you extend the legs upward. Stretch your legs really high and try to align your upper arms, hips, legs, and feet.	*This balance is difficult for many children. Don't expect mastery the first day and don't extend practice for a long time. Encourage the children with an introduction only and remind them of its difficulty. See figure 5.6.*

FIGURE 5.6   Alignment while balancing on back of shoulders, back of head, and upper arms.

COUNTERBALANCE EXTENSIONS

Learning experiences	Teaching tips
Balance on one foot by bending the knee and raising the foot off the floor. Extend both arms slowly forward, seeing how far you can extend. If you start to lose your balance, put your foot down.	*Demonstrate the stretching of the arms forward, not upward, for the extension.*
Try it again but this time as you extend the arms forward, extend your free leg behind you. Move slowly and with control. This action is called counterbalance. Extensions in one direction require extensions in the opposite direction.	
Balance on two knees, two feet, and two hands. Slowly extend one leg. Your base of support is now one knee, one foot, and two hands.	
Extend the opposite arm for a counterbalance. Your base of support is now one foot, one knee, and the opposite hand. Remember to use tight muscles and strive for stillness for three to five seconds.	
Explore other balances where you can use the extensions for counterbalance. Remember to use slow movements and tight muscles.	*If students are struggling with ideas, provide verbal suggestions or a listing on the whiteboard or screen (figure 5.7).*

 Remember, if you use the head, you must add at least three more body parts for the base of support. Hands only is not an option.

FIGURE 5.7   Extensions in opposite directions for counterbalance.

Good extensions for counterbalance.

Photo courtesy of the authors.

PARTNER COUNTERBALANCE USING COUNTER-RESISTANCE

Learning experiences	Teaching tips
Find a partner of equal size to you and stand back to back on a mat. You are going to counterbalance with your partner. You need to communicate with each other as you try the next few challenges.	*Ensure that students select partners of equal size for safety.*
Interlock arms at the elbow. Lean back and push against your partner with your upper back. Keep pushing with your back as both of you take a giant step with your right foot followed by your left foot forward, bringing it even with your right foot. Hold for three to five seconds. Slowly return one step back at a time.	*If the supply of mats is limited, place children in groups of four to take turns.*
Give your partner a high five if the two of you communicated well with each other. Raise your hand if you can tell me how you communicated.	
Communication with your partner will be important as you balance with pushing or counter-resistance with your partner. Facing your partner, balance on two knees and use counter-resistance with your partner. Explore the distance you need to be from your partner to make this activity challenging. Concentrate on keeping alignment over your base of support.	*Observe for safety and communication.*
Balance on your seat only and use your feet to push against each other for counter-resistance. You need to start with your hands on the mat. When ready, extend your arms and tighten your core muscles to help with your own counterbalance as well as the partner balance.	

PARTNER COUNTERBALANCE USING COUNTER-TENSION

Learning experiences	Teaching tips
Stand facing your partner. Grip each other's wrist on both arms. Touch toes to toes and slowly pull away by leaning backward using counter-tension to create the counterbalance. Talk to your partner as you explore the level of arm extension needed for counterbalance. Maintain the narrow shape and alignment. Do not bend at the waist; do not allow your seat to drop.	*Observe for safety and communication.* *See figure 5.8.*
Stand side by side and join inside arms in the wrist grip. Your base of support for this counter-tension balance is one foot, the foot closer to your partner. Maintain tight muscles and alignment as you lean away from your partner. Extend your free body parts while maintaining the counterbalance.	
The handout shows a variety of partner balances for counter-tension and counter-resistance. Explore those as you continue to practice with your partner.	*Distribute the handout or project it on a screen (see chapter appendix at the end of the chapter).*

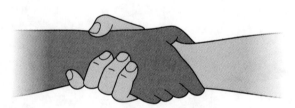

FIGURE 5.8   Wrist grip for counter-tension.

BALANCING USING BODY SHAPES AND LEVELS

The movement concepts of body shapes and levels (see chapter 4) are all applied to gymnastics. Their purposeful use adds richness to balances. The total body and body parts can create round, narrow, wide, and twisted shaped balances (figure 5.9). The whole body can be used to create symmetrical and nonsymmetrical balances (figure 5.10). The three levels are high, medium, and low. The total body is below the height of the knees for balances at a low level. Medium-level balances necessitate having most of the body at a height between the knees and shoulders, and high-level balances include at least one body part extended above shoulder height. Most balances occur at low or medium levels.

FIGURE 5.9   Balances in different body shapes.

a   *b*

FIGURE 5.10   Symmetrical *(a)* and nonsymmetrical *(b)* balances.

Balancing Shapes and Levels

Cognitive: Balances can be in wide, narrow, curled, twisted, symmetrical, and nonsymmetrical shapes. A wide base of support is more stable. Balances can be at low, medium, or high levels. Base of support, levels, and body shapes combine to make a variety of balances. Use decision-making skills to meet the criteria required.

Skills: Perform quality balances on different bases of support, at different levels, and with a variety of body shapes.

Criteria: Tight muscles, alignment, and stillness.

Safety: Personal space. Ensure that mats (if used) do not slide.

Equipment and organization: No equipment or individual small mats; students in personal space. Paper and pencil for each child.

WIDE, NARROW, CURLED, AND TWISTED SHAPES

Learning experiences	Teaching tips
Today we are going to use wide, narrow, curled, and twisted shapes in our gymnastic balances.	*Use as an introduction to the learning experiences.* *Review body shapes with the class (see chapter 4). Students should demonstrate a functional understanding, both cognitive and performance, of each of the shapes.*
Find your personal space but make sure you have a little extra space. We will call this personal space extended. Balance on two hands and two feet in a wide body shape. Do not forget tight muscles and alignment. Now, bring your hands and feet together so that they are touching or almost touching, changing your wide shape to narrow. Try each one again and tell me if one is easier than the other.	*Most will say wide is easier, but some may disagree given the simplicity of this example.*
Let's try another. Balance in a wide shape on one hand and the opposite foot. Remember to extend your free body parts to help you counterbalance. Now, try a narrow balance on one hand and the foot on the same side. Even with extensions for counterbalance, this one is more difficult. Maybe you can hold it for only one or two seconds.	
Why is this one more difficult? A wide base of support helps you distribute your weight better and keeps you more stable.	*Ask students to explain why this one is more difficult. Wait for response.*
Explore other bases of support for balancing in a wide shape and then in a narrow shape.	*Some students may need assistance on choosing the base or bases of support to explore.*
▲ **Remember, the head must have at least three other body parts for the base of support; do not attempt two hands only.**	
Balance in a curled shape on just your seat. Remember to make your body curled and hold perfectly still. Tight core or stomach muscles will help.	*Have students pat their stomach as a reminder of the core area of the body.*
Balance in a curled shape on your back.	
Balance in a curled shape on your stomach. This one is harder because your spine can only curve a little bit backward; simply try to arch your back.	*Some may find that holding their ankles helps.*
Balance on two knees, two feet, and two elbows in a curled shape.	*This balance may be too challenging for some with large midsections. Offer the option of hands instead of elbows.*

(continued)

Learning experiences	Teaching tips
Explore other options for bases of support while balancing in a curled shape.	*Check to ensure that all are doing gymnastic balances and not resting positions. Observe for a curled spine.*
Balance on two feet and one knee. Rotate your trunk to make a twisted shape. Explore other bases of support for balancing in a twisted shape. The twist can be your whole body or parts of your body.	
Challenge: Transform your body from one shape to another. Select one of the shape balances (wide, narrow, curled, or twisted) and slowly transform into another shape. You can keep the same base of support, or you can change it. Now, slowly transfer into a third shape and finally a fourth. Practice the four-shape transformation making sure you hold each balance for three to five seconds before you slowly change it. When you have it memorized, ask a partner to watch your balances for the four shapes. Your partner will name the shape as you demonstrate each balance. Change roles and repeat the challenge.	*Groups of two with one active and one assessing, taking turns.*

SYMMETRICAL AND NONSYMMETRICAL SHAPES

Learning experiences	Teaching tips
The other two body shapes are symmetrical and nonsymmetrical. Who remembers the difference between the two?	*Use as an introduction to the learning experiences.* *Expected response: Symmetrical means that both sides of your body are the same, and nonsymmetrical means that the sides are different. Demonstrate a symmetrical shape and show how a simple change makes it nonsymmetrical.*
Balance on two hands and two feet in a symmetrical shape. Slowly remove one hand or one foot, changing to a nonsymmetrical shape. Return to the symmetrical shape. Find another way to balance on two hands and two feet in a symmetrical shape. Now, make it nonsymmetrical. Return to the symmetrical shape.	*Check for understanding by asking some students if their shape is symmetrical or nonsymmetrical.*
Challenge: Balance on the back of your shoulders, back of your head, and upper arms with your legs extended upward making a symmetrical shape. Change it to a nonsymmetrical shape. Return to a symmetrical shape. Find another way to make it nonsymmetrical. Return to symmetrical.	*Some students may not be able to do a full extension of legs. Provide the option of leg position while still maintaining the requested shapes.*
Explore other balances that you can change from symmetrical to nonsymmetrical and back to symmetrical.	*Some students may need guidance.*

Nonsymmetrical balances.

Photo courtesy of the authors.

COMBINING SHAPES AND SYMMETRY

Learning experiences	Teaching tips
Now, we will combine our shapes of wide, narrow, curled, and twisted with symmetrical and nonsymmetrical. Balance in a wide shape that is symmetrical.	*Observe for symmetry as shapes change.*
Balance in a curled shape that is nonsymmetrical.	
Balance in a narrow shape that is symmetrical.	
Balance in a twisted shape. Would the twisted balance be symmetrical or nonsymmetrical?	*Wait on response of nonsymmetrical.*

BALANCING AT DIFFERENT LEVELS

Learning experiences	Teaching tips
In personal space, stand on the balls of your feet and reach for the ceiling, extending both arms as high as you can stretch. This high-level balance may be challenging for some of you. Remember to try for stillness for three to five seconds.	*Point to the ball of one foot as you demonstrate.* *If this balance appears easy for some, challenge them to balance more on the toes and less on the ball of the foot.*
Repeat the balance, focusing on body alignment from feet, to hips, to shoulders, and even to your fingers.	
Create a high-level balance with only one foot as your base of support.	
Balance on two hands and two feet at a low level. Remember, low level is below knee height. As I walk around, I will see if you are lower than my knees.	*Observe for bodies extended with balance on two hands and two feet to ensure low level, not medium.*
Balance on one hand and two feet and extend the free arm, being sure to keep it at low level.	
Explore low-level balances with changes of your bases of support. Concentrate on quality balances with tight muscles and alignment.	*Observe for levels and quality. Some students may need guidance.*
For a medium level, your base of support will still be at a low level while placing some of your body at medium level. Remember that medium level is between your knees and shoulder height. Repeat the balance you did at a low level on two hands and two feet but see how you can adjust your body to make this a medium-level balance.	*Observe and comment that the task requires simply bringing hands closer to feet.*
Explore other medium-level balances with changes in your bases of support. After three to five seconds, try a different one. Focus on tight muscles and good extensions.	*If students are struggling with ideas, provide verbal suggestions or post examples on the whiteboard or screen.*

Learning experiences	Teaching tips
Balance on two feet and one hand at a low level. With the same base of support, balance at a medium level. Explore other balances where the same base of support works for low- and medium-level balances. Remember to use tight muscles and hold for three to five seconds before creating another. As I walk around, I will ask you to tell me the level of your balance.	*Observe the children's work and check for cognitive as well as performance understanding because some students may attempt balances without the cognitive involvement you are requesting.*
Challenge: Balance on the back of your shoulders, back of your head, and your upper arms. Tighten those core or stomach muscles and curl your body, balancing at a low level. Now, slowly raise your legs into a medium level. Tighten the muscles for a three- to five-second count. Slowly extend your legs and point your toes. You are now performing a high-level balance.	*Concentrated work is exhausting for children; rest breaks are an excellent time for cognitive review. Not all children will be able to do the high-level balance. Encourage and then allow continual practice of medium level with different leg positions.*

Balance on two hands and two feet at a medium level.

Photo courtesy of the authors.

COMBINING SHAPES AND LEVELS

Learning experiences	Teaching tips
The next several balances are a chance for you to combine all you have learned about balancing. You will get to show off your favorites. Remember to focus on quality balance with stillness, tight muscles, alignment, and, when needed, counterbalance.	*Use as an introduction to the learning experiences.* *On a whiteboard or projected on a screen, list in three columns the levels, bases of support, and body shapes.*
🔺 **Remember, if you use your head as part of the base of support, you must use at least three other body parts.**	
Choose three balances each with a different base of support, all at low level. After three to five seconds, stay at low level and change your base of support until you have performed all three.	*Inform students to reference the first two columns (levels and bases) and remind them that they may have other options for the base of support.*
Using the same or a different base of support, choose three balances at a low level, each with a different body shape. They can be wide, narrow, curled, or twisted.	*Inform students they are now including the third column of shapes.*
Create three balances, each with a different base of support at medium level. Remember that good extensions will help you make medium-level balances. After three to five seconds, change your base of support until you have performed all three.	
Using the same or a different base of support, choose three balances at a medium level, each with a different body shape. Select three of the four body shapes: wide, narrow, curled, or twisted. After three to five seconds, change your body shape until you have performed at least three of the four body shapes.	
Create two balances at a high level. To make each one different, change either the base of support or body shape. Remember that for high level, at least one body part must be at a high level. After three to five seconds, change from one to the next. .	

Learning experiences	Teaching tips
Challenge: Select three different balances, each of which must have a different level, base of support, and body shape. Choose one from each column for all three balances. Explore for a few minutes to decide on your three balances.	
Now, you will combine the three balances. Determine an order you think is best to connect your three balances. Move slowly from one balance to the next after holding each for three to five seconds. You will end with a "Ta-da." Make sure your last balance allows you to move into the ending "Ta-da." Practice until you know it is your best and you have it memorized. On your piece of paper, write or draw your combination listing the level, base of support, and body shape of each.	*Ask a child to demonstrate the "Ta-da." Provide paper and pencils for students to write or draw their selections listing the base, shape, and level.* *Allow time for decision making, writing, and practice.*
You are going to pretend you are performing in a halftime show of a high school basketball game. This half of the room will watch while this half performs. Then you will change roles. When it is your turn to perform, I will ask for your first balance and then count to 3 Mississippi. You will slowly change to your second balance, 3 Mississippi, your third balance, 3 Mississippi, and the ending "Ta-da." After the three balances and the ending "Ta-da," spectators can clap.	*Divide the class in half; one group performs and then the other.*

Summary

At the conclusion of these foundational learning experiences, the students will have a functional understanding of the principles of balance. In essence, they will have the knowledge and body control to be able to demonstrate a variety of quality balances with stillness, changes in base of support, muscular tension, weight distribution, body alignment, extension of free body parts, counterbalance, and use of wide bases of support. They will also have a repertoire of balances they can perform in wide, narrow, curled, twisted, symmetrical, and nonsymmetrical body shapes as well as high, medium, and low levels.

In chapter 6, students will be introduced to inverted balances. With body control established from the learning experiences in this chapter, students will be ready to explore weight transfer actions such as stretching, twisting, curling, and rolling and the in-flight actions of locomotors, jumping, and hands-feet-hands travel. The weight transfer actions will be used to connect balances and create and perform individual and partner sequences.

Appendix

COUNTERBALANCE CHALLENGES

From T.J. Hall and S.A. Holt/Hale, *Educational Gymnastics for Children* (Champaign, IL: Human Kinetics, 2024).

Zave Smith/Stone/Getty Images

Balance and Weight Transfer

The learning experiences in chapter 5 provided the foundation for body awareness and body control essential for good balance. These foundational skills and concepts are prerequisites for the more complex balance and weight transfer learning experiences in this chapter. The primary focus at this junction is to combine balance and weight transfer. The learning experiences are interwoven as they are in the teaching of educational gymnastics.

The expectations of the quality and variety from previously learned balances continue and inverted balances are introduced. For weight transference the focus turns to how the body weight is moved from one balance or position to another. The weight transfer emphasis starts with an introduction to basic sideways and safety shoulder rolls and continues with the transitional movements between two points of support including stretching, twisting, curling, and rolling actions. In-flight actions wherein the body is momentarily airborne are introduced next and include locomotors, jumping and landing, and feet-hands-feet travel.

Body shapes and levels continue as experiences to enhance balances and are introduced in weight transfer actions; both are related to many weight transfer actions. For example, a rolling action may be in a narrow or curled shape. Wide, twisted, or narrow shapes can be explored when transferring weight from feet to hands to feet. A symmetrical body shape may change to nonsymmetrical as weight transfers between balances. Examples of levels in weight transfer include a narrow roll sideways at a low level, a weight transfer from feet to hands to feet, beginning and ending at either a medium or a high level, and shapes in flight at a high level.

Mini Index for Learning Experiences

Weight Transfer Rolling 89
   Rolling Sideways in Narrow and Curled Body Shapes. 90
      Narrow Rolls Sideways 90
      Curled Rolls Sideways 92

Rolling Over the Shoulders 92

    Safety Shoulder Roll Forward 93

    Safety Shoulder Roll Backward 94

Inverted Balances 96

  Balancing in a Variety of Inverted Positions 97

    Introduction to Inverted Balances 97

    Safety Review 98

    Two Hands and Head as Bases of Support 99

Weight Transference Between Balances 102

  Out of and Into Balances With Stretching, Twisting, Curling, and Rolling Actions 102

    Out of Balances With a Stretching or Twisting Action 103

    Out of Balances With a Curling, Rolling Action 105

    Out of Inverted Balances With Narrow and Curled Rolling Actions 107

Weight Transference With Levels and Shapes 109

  Transfers Between Balances, Different Levels and Shapes 109

    Low Level, Shapes and Transfers 109

    Medium Level, Shapes and Transfers 110

    High Level, Shapes and Transfers 111

    Using Transfers to Change Level of Balances 112

    Using Transfers to Change Shapes of Balances 112

    Using Transfers to Change Symmetrical and Nonsymmetrical Balances 114

Weight Transference Using In-Flight Actions 115

  Locomotors and Other Actions With Balances 115

    Exploring Different Movements With Locomotors 116

    Combining Locomotors With Balances 117

  Jumping High With Turns and Shapes, Combining Balances 117

    Review of Jumping From Two Feet to Two Feet and One Foot to Two Feet 118

    Shapes in the Air: Wide, Narrow, Curled 119

    Shapes in the Air: Symmetrical and Nonsymmetrical 120

    Jumps and Turns 121

    Jumps and Balances 122

  Transferring Weight Feet-Hands-Feet 122

    Taking Weight on Hands Momentarily 123

    Weight Transfer Feet-Hands-Feet With Twisting Action 125

    Weight Transfer Feet-Hands-Feet With Wheel Action 126

    Combine Balances and Feet-Hands-Feet Transfers 127

Educational Gymnastics Sequences 128

  Creating Individual Sequences 128

  Individual Sequences in Action 129

    Review of Balance and Weight Transfer Combinations 130

    Individual Sequence Creation and Performance 131

  Creating Partner Sequences 131

  Partner Sequences in Action 132

    Partner Relationships 132

    Partner Sequence Creation and Performance 134

WEIGHT TRANSFER ROLLING

Transferring weight by rolling is primarily done in a curled, round body shape. A functional understanding of a curled body shape inclusive of head tucked with chin on chest is critical for quality rolls and, most important, safety. The head is an extension of the spine and as such must be included as part of the curve made by the rest of the body. In traditional gymnastics, curled rolls include forward rolls, backward rolls, sideways rolls (sometimes called egg rolls), and safety shoulder rolls, both forward and backward. The traditional forward roll or backward roll should not be taught to all children in school physical education programs. Having children perform either of these rolls without the prerequisite upper-body strength and manageable body weight as well as proper training for the physical education teacher is not safe.

Another rolling option, and often a favorite of young children, is sideways in a stretched, narrow shape. Visualize the thrill a child has rolling in a narrow shape down a hill. In traditional gymnastics, this roll is called a log or pencil roll.

Sideways rolls and forward and backward safety shoulder rolls are important components of gymnastics for children and should be taught before work on balances with transfers. The forward safety shoulder roll is a safety prerequisite for learning inverted balances; thus, it is taught at this point in the gymnastics progression. The following learning experiences include sideways rolls narrow and curled, and safety shoulder rolls forward and backward.

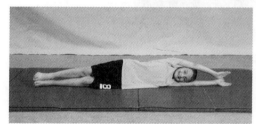 

Rolling sideways narrow body shape.

Rolling sideways curled body shape.

Rolling Sideways in Narrow and Curled Body Shapes

Cognitive: Body shapes must be maintained throughout rolls. Tight muscles help maintain body shapes.

Skills: Roll sideways in a narrow shape; roll sideways in a curled shape.

Criteria: Narrow body shape with arms extended, head between arms, and total body alignment. Roll begins by leading with the hips. Curled body shape with head tucked chin to chest, legs and arms bent near the body. Rolling smoothly to the right and left sides while tightening muscles and maintaining body shape.

Safety: Awareness of others, ability to keep body and head in required body shape throughout the roll. Taking turns on mat.

Equipment and organization: Scattered individual mats or enough large mats for children to work safely.

NARROW ROLLS SIDEWAYS

Learning experiences	Teaching tips
Earlier in the year you learned four body shapes: wide, narrow, curled, twisted. Tell your neighbor which of those shapes you think is best for rolling. If you heard "curled," you heard correctly. You can also roll with a narrow shape.	*Use as an introduction to the lesson before sending to the mats.*
Lie on the end of your mat in a narrow body shape and roll the length of your mat. Picture a log or a pencil rolling.	*Observation of students rolling will reveal that their rolls tend to be crooked rather than straight.*
Only one person will be rolling at a time. When one person is off, the next person may start. This procedure is critical for safety.	
Share with all students as one student demonstrates: • Starting position is lying on the end of the mat in a narrow body shape with arms stretched above your head. • Your head should be in the center of your arms and should stay there throughout the roll. • Tighten all your muscles from toes to tips of fingers. Make sure that the core muscles in your stomach area are extra tight. • Keeping those tight core muscles, allow your hips to lead as you roll over your stomach and continue to your back. The roll continues sideways.	*A focus on the critical elements for rolling sideways in a narrow shape will be needed with demonstration and practice by the class. Select one student for a demonstration as you talk through the critical elements (figure 6.1).* *When demonstrating on a mat, make sure that all students can see and hear.*

Learning experiences	Teaching tips
Roll the length of the mat with a narrow shape, demonstrating all the critical elements of the narrow shape side roll. Return to start by rolling the opposite direction. Repeat the rolls and this time focus on tight muscles and allowing your hips to lead the roll.	*As students return to the mats for practice, focus on one or two of the critical elements. Observe the practice and introduce another critical element when students are ready.*
Challenge: Try the narrow roll again but this time with arms by your sides. Lead with your hips and maintain tight muscles.	*Provide the challenge for students who are ready. Others may continue practicing with arms stretched above head.*

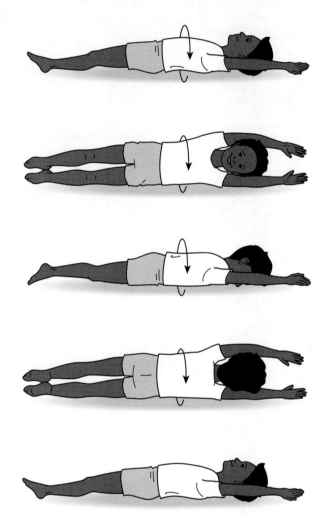

FIGURE 6.1   Rolling sideways in a narrow body shape.

CURLED ROLLS SIDEWAYS

Learning experiences	Teaching tips
Lie on your mat in a curled shape, making sure you have space to the right and to the left. You should look like a ball.	*If students are sharing a mat, a child can be at each end.*
Tuck your chin to your chest and hold those knees in tight. Rock from one side to another. Use your core stomach muscles and your arms around your knees to stay in the curled shape.	
This time rock a little faster using your momentum to help you roll over your stomach and continue to your back one time. Do not raise your chin as you roll. Continue practicing.	*See figure 6.2.*
Slowly roll the length of your mat maintaining the curled body shape, chin on chest, and tight muscles. If needed, start with a rocking motion. Reverse and roll the other direction.	*If sharing a mat, remind students to return to one at a time.*
Challenge: In starting position, place elbows close to your sides instead of arms around your legs. Rolling sideways with arms not around your legs will require you to use really tight core muscles. Slowly roll the length of your mat maintaining the curled body shape, chin on chest, and tight muscles. Reverse and roll back.	*Provide the challenge for students who are ready. Others may continue practicing while holding their knees.*

FIGURE 6.2   Rolling sideways in a curled body shape.

Rolling Over the Shoulders

Cognitive: Curled body shape must be maintained throughout rolls. The head is an extension of your spine and is therefore critical to the curl. Chin on chest is required for the curl. Tight muscles help maintain body shapes.

Skills: Roll over shoulder, forward and backward, in curled body shape.

Criteria: Tuck chin on chest, curl body, lean to one side. Soft rolling action, maintaining curled shape. *Forward safety shoulder roll*: Stretch arm under body on side you plan to roll followed by a twisting action, allowing shoulder to make soft contact. *Backward safety shoulder roll*: Extend the arm on the same side as the roll and lean your opposite ear toward the shoulder.

Safety: Awareness of others and ability to keep body and head in required body shape throughout the roll. Taking turns on mat.

Equipment and organization: Scattered individual mats or enough large mats for children to work safely.

SAFETY SHOULDER ROLL FORWARD

Learning experiences	Teaching tips
The next roll is called a safety shoulder roll because it is a safe way to roll if you lose your balance. This roll is also used in many martial arts.	*Use as an introduction to the lesson before sending to the mats. Connect to specific martial arts, ninjas, video games, and movies.*
Share with all students as one student demonstrates: The roll is in a curled shape and can be performed over either shoulder. • Starting position is balancing on your hands, knees, and feet with your spine curled at one end of the mat. • Tuck your chin on chest to complete the curl. • Last, stretch one arm between your opposite arm and leg while you lower the shoulder and roll.	*Demonstrate or have a child demonstrate as you describe the action (see figure 6.3). When demonstrating on a mat be sure that all students can see and hear. Review sharing of mat if necessary.*
Return to your mat as I talk you through these steps again.	*Repeat the action steps stated in the demonstration.*
Continue practicing with a focus on chin on chest and curled shape. The roll should be smooth with soft contact on the mat. Keep the curled body shape until the finish. When you feel comfortable, try rolling over the other shoulder.	*Some children overthink this skill and struggle with starting the roll. Provide guidance as needed. Peer assistance is also helpful.*
Challenge: Try the safety shoulder roll from a squatting position. Keep the chin on chest and stretch the arm on the same side of the roll through the opposite arm and body opening as you lower your shoulder. This time, push with your feet as you drop your shoulder. The roll should still be smooth with only soft mat contact. The momentum you create from your feet should bring you back to your feet. Maintain the curled shape from feet to feet.	*Some children do better from this position as the feet can produce more momentum than the knees. Encourage students to attempt this challenge with the understanding they can return to the previous starting position.*
Advanced challenge: Try the safety shoulder roll from a medium-level stance. Balance on two feet, shoulder-width apart, with knees bent and lower your body as you lean forward into the shoulder roll. Try to roll fast enough to return to a stand.	*Students who have mastered the previous roll are ready to attempt this roll, with a return to their feet.*

FIGURE 6.3 Safety shoulder roll forward.

SAFETY SHOULDER ROLL BACKWARD

Learning experiences	Teaching tips
Next, you will try the backward shoulder roll. Some of you may find it easier. To make it easier, I am going to present this roll one part at a time. When we have it all together, it will look like this. Return to your mats.	*Take the students to one mat for a demonstration.* *The backward shoulder roll is best learned in the step-by-step approach in the learning experiences. Demonstrate or use a video to show the full action first. See figure 6.4.*
Lie on your back in a curled shape, chin tucked to chest, knees to chest, arms holding your legs—the same as when you rocked sideways. Rock backward, keeping your curled shape. Try to rock from shoulders to feet in a continual motion. Keep the core muscles tight.	*Demonstrate each step and allow practice time before moving to the next step.*
Try rocking again but do not hold your legs. You must really use those tight core muscles to keep your knees in. Remember to keep your chin and knees tucked.	
Balance in the squat position with your back to the mat. Make a curled body shape with hands on floor in front of you and chin tucked on chest. Lean forward and then rock backward, keeping the curled shape. Use your tight core muscles to stay curled; do not hold your legs. Keeping the chin tucked, rock back to shoulders and return to seat. Do not allow your body to roll over yet.	
Challenge: Rock backward, with enough momentum to rock back to shoulders and return to feet.	*When demonstrating, emphasize that a faster rocking motion is needed.*
You are ready to try the backward safety shoulder roll. The arm position can be a little confusing. Let's focus on it first. Stand and face me. Extend your right arm out to the side. Tuck your chin and tilt your head, almost placing your ear on the left shoulder. Your ear goes toward your shoulder, not your shoulder to your ear. Your left hand should be in the same position as when you rocked. What you have created is an opening to roll over the right shoulder.	*Remember that when facing the class you are in a mirror position. If students extend the right arm, you will extend your left arm.*
Try this same position from the backward squat position. Make your curled shape with the chin tucked; keep that position. On my signal, extend the right arm to the side and place the left hand beside your head. At the same time, lean your ear toward the left shoulder. Try it a few times to coordinate this movement. Make sure you are staying curled.	

Learning experiences	Teaching tips
Share with all students as one student demonstrates:	*Bring the students to one mat for a demonstration.*
• Balance in the curled backward squat position.	*Use a student to demonstrate or show a video of the whole action as you point out the steps.*
• Lean forward and then push with your legs and arms; rock back, keeping chin on chest in a round shape.	
• As you rock back extend the right arm and lean your ear to the left.	
• As your shoulders touch the mat, slightly twist your body and roll over the right shoulder.	
Return to your mat to practice; make sure you stay rounded and keep the chin tucked. Remember that a flat body will not roll. Practice until you feel comfortable with the rolling action. When ready, try to roll over the left shoulder. Practice to discover which side is your favorite.	*Watch for students losing the round shape because this is a common error.*
Challenge: Can you get enough momentum to come to your feet? Start in a balanced squat position on your feet, roll backward over shoulder of choice, and end on your feet in either a squat or a standing position. Keeping the curled shape by using tight muscles is critical.	*Provide the challenge for students who are ready. Others may continue practicing the preceding rolling action.*

FIGURE 6.4   Safety shoulder roll backward.

INVERTED BALANCES

Previous balance experiences provided opportunities for children to explore their limitations and perhaps challenge themselves as they placed their bodies in positions that they may not have experienced outside of physical education class. Inverted balances bring a new quest as the body orientation changes. Inverted balances are defined as any balance in which the head is lower than the trunk or a balance in which the head is touching the mat (figure 6.5). For most of these balances the head will be one part of the base of support; a mat is recommended.

In the previous balances, students have been encouraged to use their head with at least three additional body parts. When students can successfully perform the safety shoulder roll, they can progress to using only two additional body parts when using the head. In traditional gymnastics a balance on head and two hands is typically referred to as a tripod (knees on elbows) or a headstand. Balances on two hands and head are advanced balances. Individual students will need to demonstrate readiness before independent practice of these skills. Do not give any hint that these are preferred or superior skills. Emphasize that children should work at their individual levels of readiness.

 Review the forward safety shoulder roll before starting inverted balances. As with all work in educational gymnastics, students should not feel compelled to attempt challenges beyond their comfort zone.

FIGURE 6.5   Sample inverted balances, simple and complex.

Balancing in a Variety of Inverted Positions

Cognitive: A balance is inverted if the head is lower than the trunk or the head is touching the mat.

Skills: Demonstrate a variety of inverted balances.

Criteria: Head lower than most of the body, tight muscles.

Safety: Personal space. Ensure that mats do not slide. Safely come out of an inverted balance. Returning to feet is the best option. If that is not possible, a roll is the next option. The safety forward shoulder roll is a prerequisite skill for an inverted balance on head and two hands.

Equipment and organization: Scattered individual mats or enough large mats for children to work safely.

INTRODUCTION TO INVERTED BALANCES

Learning experiences	Teaching tips
You have learned all the qualities of a good balance, have tried numerous body parts for base of support, and can balance in different body shapes and at all three levels. You are now ready for inverted balances. An inverted balance is upside down; your head is lower than your trunk or is touching the mat.	*Use as an introduction to the lesson before sending students to the mats. Review the qualities of a good balance with students, describing each. Post them on the whiteboard or screen.*
Was my first balance inverted? What about the second one? What made it qualify as an inverted balance?	*Demonstrate two balances that will show how a balance becomes inverted. For example, balance on two hands and two feet in a narrow shape with your head raised. Then, walk your hands and feet closer together and balance on two hands and two feet, bottom up and head down with your body in a curled shape.*
In your personal space, balance on two hands and two feet in a narrow body shape. Try to distribute your weight evenly on your hands and feet. Now, adjust your body where you keep the same base of support, but your bottom is up and head is down, without head touching the mat.	*If students are sharing mats, make sure that they have ample personal space to work safely. If not, they will need to take turns.*
Now, gently touch your head to the mat. Your arms and legs are strong, so they should hold your body. Your head should support very little of your weight when four or more body parts serve as your bases of support. Focus on tight muscles and alignment. Repeat the same base of support in a wide shape. Remember that most of your weight is on your hands and feet.	
Practice the following balances as I name the bases of support for each. Stay within your comfort zone; do not try a balance unless you feel ready to do so. You can add an additional body part to the base of support for any of them. • One hand, two feet, head. Extend your free arm to counterbalance. • Two hands, one foot, head. Extend your free leg to counterbalance. • Two feet, two knees, head. Extend both arms. • Knees, elbows, head. • Knees, hands, head. • Back of your shoulders, back of your head, and upper arms. You may make a narrow, wide, or curled shape with your legs. Repeat this one, making a different shape with your legs.	*For the child-centered approach, allow students the option to add another base of support if needed.* *Allow students time to explore the balance but not so much time that they fatigue. Generally, 15 seconds is sufficient before announcing the next balance.* *See figure 6.6.*

(continued)

Learning experiences	Teaching tips
Challenge: Two feet, two hands, stomach to the sky. Arch your back with your head down but not touching the mat.	*A stick figure illustration or a demonstration of the balance will assist children in their understanding of the balance. Students not ready for this challenge can practice any of the previous inverted balances.*

FIGURE 6.6   Variety of balances on back of head, back of shoulders, and arms.

SAFETY REVIEW

Learning experiences	Teaching tips
As I observe you practicing the inverted balances, I think we need a review of the safety requirements for inverted balances.	*Call students to one mat for safety review.*
• If you lose your balance, what body parts are your first choice to return to?	• *Wait for answer of feet.*
• If you start to tip over and cannot regain your balance, what do you think you do?	• *Wait for answer of roll.*
Remember that you will need to tuck your chin, curl your body, push with your hands, and roll. You have practiced a safety shoulder roll, and we called it a safety roll for this purpose. Crashing to the mat is not an option.	*Demonstrate the forward and backward safety rolls, reviewing the critical elements.*
Return to your mats and practice the forward and backwards safety rolls.	*Watch for any students who need assistance for correct safety rolling. If mats are shared, remind them to take turns.*

Inverted balances.

Photo (left) courtesy of the authors.

TWO HANDS AND HEAD AS BASES OF SUPPORT

Learning experiences	Teaching tips
For this balance your base of support is two hands and your head. You need to distribute your weight evenly over your head and two hands; you must maintain this triangle. Your hands are shoulder-width apart with fingers spread. Return to your mat, and we will try a few balances to help you progress to the two hands and head as the base of support.	*Bring students to a mat for demonstration. Draw a triangle on the whiteboard or screen that connects two Xs and a circle. The Xs represent hands, and the circle represents the head (see figure 6.7).* *Student understanding of the triangle spacing is crucial for success. Display illustrations of the balances or have a child demonstrate as you share the critical placement of hands and head.*
Balance on two hands, two knees, two feet, and your head. Place your hands and head in the triangle. All movements from this point are slow! Tighten your arms, shoulders, and core muscles as you slowly raise your knees and rest them on or near your elbows. Focus on the tight muscles and try to align your hips over your shoulders. This balance may take several tries. Your goal is stillness in the balance for three to five seconds.	*Provide the option to try just one knee at a time.* **If the child does not have the prerequisite skills or is uncomfortable with these inverted balances, assure them that it is fine to continue working on previous inverted balances.**
Challenge: Choose a starting position balanced on head, hands, and feet or balanced on head and hands with knees on elbows. Slowly attempt to raise your legs, keeping your knees bent. Use tight muscles and attempt to align your hips over your shoulders. Do not worry about leg position yet. **Remember to tuck and roll if you start to fall over.**	*For students not ready for this challenge, encourage them to explore other inverted balances that include the head and two hands plus one more base of support.*

(continued)

Learning experiences	Teaching tips
Advanced challenge: Choose a starting position balanced on head, hands, and feet or balanced on head and hands with knees on elbows. Slowly extend legs upward to a full extension of the legs in a narrow body shape. Either approach will require concentration on tight muscles throughout your body and alignment of hips over shoulders, knees over hips, and feet over knees. Stretch your toes toward the ceiling.	*This challenge is for those who successfully completed the previous challenge and were able to hold it for three to five seconds. Inform them that you must "check them off" (observe their success) before they can attempt this advanced challenge.*
Challenge: Balance on your head and two hands and explore different positions for the placement of your legs.	*See figure 6.8.* *For students not ready for this challenge, encourage them to touch one foot or knee to the ground and explore different positions for the other leg.*

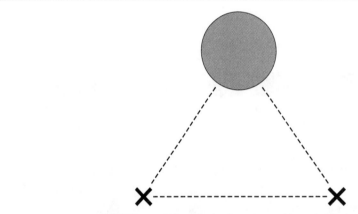

FIGURE 6.7 Triangle for hands and head relationship.

FIGURE 6.8 Variety of balances on head and two hands.

Balances on two hands and head.

WEIGHT TRANSFERENCE BETWEEN BALANCES

When students first work on balances in gymnastics, they do one balance and then another balance, giving little thought as to the transition between the balances. With the foundation of balancing on different bases of support, in inverted positions, at all three levels, and in a variety of body shapes, the students are ready to learn how to connect balances with weight transfers. Transition is an important part of gymnastics for students' beginning work, for the challenges as skills advance, for sequences, and for work on gymnastics equipment and apparatus. The transfer of weight between balances includes a focus on smoothness and flow of the movement, and, as always, safety. Some transfers are a natural transition, some require concentration, and others are awkward or disjointed, that is, they just don't fit. The idea is body control from start to finish. Students need guided and independent practice time for discovery of the transfer out of and into a balance. Bases of support and levels for balances are important factors in determining the best connection of transfer to balance. Students should be encouraged to focus on quality transitional actions as well as quality balances. As always, variety is encouraged.

Stretching, twisting, and curling actions play a big role in transfer out of and into balances. Students will benefit from a review of these (see chapter 4). The sideways rolls in narrow and round shapes and the safety shoulder roll forward and backward are added skills that students can use as transfers. Review the rolls and previous learning experiences such as balance on different bases of support and inverted balance before beginning the transfer learning experiences.

Out of and Into Balances With Stretching, Twisting, Curling, and Rolling Actions

Cognitive: Stretching, twisting, curling, and rolling actions can move the body out of and into balances. Transitions are smooth, flowing actions. Exploration and decision making are required to determine which actions are best for smooth, flowing transitions from one balance to another.

Skills: Transfer out of and into balances with stretching, twisting, curling, and rolling actions.

Criteria: Transfer smoothly from one balance into another balance while selecting the suitable stretching, twisting, curling, or rolling action. Quality rolls and balances.

Safety: Personal space, awareness of others, reminder that when using head, at least two body parts must be included, and review of safety shoulder roll before performing inverted balances.

Equipment and organization: Scattered individual mats or enough large mats for children to work safely.

OUT OF BALANCES WITH A STRETCHING OR TWISTING ACTION

Learning experiences	Teaching tips
For the next few learning experiences, you will be moving from one balance to another using stretching or twisting actions. Begin with a balance on one foot, stretching arms high above your head.	*Students need expanded personal space on mats (sufficient space for children to transfer weight out of and into balances). If space is not available, remind students of safety rules for taking turns.*

For the next few learning experiences, you will be moving from one balance to another using stretching or twisting actions. Begin with a balance on one foot, stretching arms high above your head.

Students need expanded personal space on mats (sufficient space for children to transfer weight out of and into balances). If space is not available, remind students of safety rules for taking turns.

Slowly move the arms from high level to medium level, stretching them forward as the free leg extends backward for counterbalance.

Hold for three to five seconds and then slowly extend the arms forward and downward to low level—farther, farther, until you begin to lose your balance. This stretching action will result in the body being off balance and you will transfer to one foot and two hands as the new base of support. Focus on a smooth transition to the new base of support, not a collapse.

Try it again on the other foot.

Balance on two knees, two feet, and one hand. Extend the free arm toward medium level.

Change your base of support to one hand and the opposite knee and foot as you extend the opposite leg for counterbalance.

Slowly stretch the free arm under the body reaching beyond the body on the opposite side. As the arm stretches and the body twists, slowly lower the body and touch your shoulder to floor or mat. The new base of support is one hand, one knee, one foot, and your shoulder. Hold that position for three to five seconds.

Balance on two feet and two hands with stomach facing the sky.

Raise one arm and extend across the body, twisting the trunk as the foot elevates and extends across the body with the arm. Continue the stretching and twisting action until the body moves into a new balance on two feet and two hands with stomach facing the floor. Remember to try for smooth transitions and stillness of balances. Tight muscles will help you move slowly.

Balance on one foot with absolute stillness.

Observe and reinforce slow movements.

Rotate the trunk and slowly move the arms across and around the body to create a twisting action. Continue the twisting action until you are off balance and your weight transfers momentarily to both feet and then on to the other foot for a new balance. Hold for three to five seconds.

Remember that you can use your arms and free leg for counterbalance.

Repeat the one foot and twist action, but this time, as you twist, lower your body to a new balance on the opposite foot and two hands.

(continued)

Learning experiences	Teaching tips
Balanced on shoulders, back of your head, and upper arms, stretch the legs upward as high as you are comfortable. Hold for three to five seconds.	
Twist the lower torso and bring the legs down to a new position, one or both feet to the floor. Your new base of support is shoulders, back of head, arms, and one or two feet.	*The location of where the foot (feet) touch will be based on the child's flexibility. The location is up to them.*
Be careful not to overextend backward over the head because that movement is unsafe.	
Explore stretching and twisting actions you can safely use to connect one balance to a new balance. Hold each balance for three to five seconds using tight muscles. The stretching or twisting transition should flow smoothly from one balance to another. Try each one twice. The first time is to create the transfer. The second time is a focus on a smooth-flowing transition.	*Observe for safety and provide individual assistance as needed for students struggling with the task.* *See figure 6.9.*
If you chose to use an inverted balance, remember our safety tips. If you should start to lose balance, the best option is to come to your feet. The second option is to curl, tuck your chin, and use a safety roll. **Remember the head plus two rule. Always have at least two other body parts in support when the head is a base of support.**	
Challenge: Select your favorite balance and use a twisting or stretching transition action into a new balance you have performed today. Ask someone working next to you to observe for a twisting or stretching action and two different balances with stillness.	*If students are not sharing a mat, combine into partners.*

FIGURE 6.9 Sample using stretching actions to transition balances.

OUT OF BALANCES WITH A CURLING, ROLLING ACTION

Learning experiences	Teaching tips
Now you are ready to add rolling actions as transfers. Some of your transfers will include the stretching and twisting actions that you just practiced. Those actions can lead into a roll.	
Take a few minutes to review your sideways curled roll and the forward and backward shoulder rolls. Remember that your spine is curled and your chin is to the chest for all three rolls.	*Review all three rolls, providing critical elements as needed.*
Balance on two knees and two hands, extending one arm under and across your body as you twist the trunk. Continue this stretching and twisting action until you are off balance, curling the body and rolling to the side, ending in a balance on two knees and one hand. Practice that balance and transition with the curling action to the right and the curling action to the left.	*Weight transfers with a curling action (rolling) need to be at low level, either out of a balance that is at low level or after the body has transitioned to low level for the action.* *Emphasize quality in both the balances and the rolls.*
Balance on your seat with arms and legs extended. Curl the spine as you rock back, tuck the arms and legs to the chest; roll sideways into a balance on two hands and two feet, facing ceiling. Extend the arms and legs using tight muscles.	*See figure 6.10.*
For the next curling action, you are going to review a previous balance that used a stretching and twisting transition into a new balance. Balance on two knees and one hand. Extend the free arm toward medium level, change your base of support to one hand and the opposite knee as you extend the opposite leg for counterbalance. Slowly stretch the free arm under the body reaching beyond the body on the opposite side. As the arm stretches and the body twists, slowly lower and curl the body, and touch your shoulder to the mat. The new base of support is one hand, one knee, and your shoulder. Hold that position for three to five seconds.	
Repeat the preceding action but as you lower the shoulder to the mat, tuck the chin, curling the body and transferring out of the balance with a safety roll. The rolling action is with the shoulder and back, not the head; tuck the head and curl the spine as you roll. End in a balance of your choice.	🚧 ***Emphasize that this is a safety roll to the side, not a forward roll.***

(continued)

Learning experiences	Teaching tips
Balance on two knees and one hand. Curl your body and roll over your shoulder, ending in a balance with your seat and one foot as the bases of support.	*Focus on quality balances with tight muscles and good extensions of free body parts.*
Remember to keep chin on chest and stay round through your safety shoulder roll. Control your speed as you transfer weight into the second balance.	
Repeat, alternating right and left shoulders; each time try a different base of support for the balance after the roll. If you are not comfortable with the safety shoulder roll, you may continue to use the curled sideways roll.	
Balance on two feet and two hands in a squat position. Transfer weight using a safety shoulder roll and end in a balance on your seat and one foot. Practice until the transition is smooth.	
Challenge: Balance on two feet and two hands in a squat position. Transfer weight using a safety shoulder roll and end in a balance on two feet and one hand. For this one, you need to speed up your roll by pushing with your feet and hands.	*Students not ready for this challenge may explore other ending balances.*
Advanced challenge: Balance on two feet and bend your knees, placing your body at a medium level. Transfer weight using a safety shoulder roll, returning to two feet. Extend your arms and one foot, balancing on one foot.	*This advanced challenge is only for students who have shown you that they can complete a shoulder roll from the medium-level starting position.*

FIGURE 6.10 Sample balance, roll, balance.

OUT OF INVERTED BALANCES WITH NARROW AND CURLED ROLLING ACTIONS

Learning experiences	Teaching tips
Let's try inverted balances with curling and rolling transfers. To be considered an inverted balance, the head must be lower than the trunk or touching the mat.	*Remind students of safety when sharing mats and the rule of not balancing on hands only.*
Remember the head plus two rule. Always have at least two other body parts supporting when the head is in use. **The head is never used alone as a base of support for a balance. If you feel unsafe when using your head, push with the arms to lift the head slightly off the mat, tuck your chin, and roll to the side or over the shoulder.**	
On your mat, practice your favorite inverted balances.	
Balance on two hands and one foot. Extend the free foot to a high level and lower your head. Maintain stillness for three to five seconds and then lower your body, tuck your chin, and roll over the shoulder opposite the free foot. End in a balance of your choice.	
Balance on one knee, one foot, two hands, and your head. Lower the body to the mat and slowly roll to the side with the body either stretched into a narrow shape or curled for a rounded shape. Transition into a balance on two hands and two feet.	*See figure 6.11.*
Balance on your knees, elbows, and head. Tuck your chin, curl your body, and roll sideways into a balance on two feet and one hand.	
Balance on two knees, two hands, and your head. Curl the spine and tuck your chin as you transfer weight to the total body in a curled shape. Roll to the side, extend the body, and stretch into a balance on stomach or back.	
Balance on one hand, two feet, and head. Extend your free arm to counterbalance. Stretch your free arm under your body, curl, and roll, using either a side roll or safety shoulder roll. Transition to a balance of your choice.	
Challenge: Balance on two knees, two hands, and your head. Raise your knees and place them on your upper arms or elbows, balancing on hands and head only. Hold for three to five seconds. Transfer back to the bases of support of knees, hands, and head. Roll to the side into a new balance of your choice.	*Students not ready for this challenge can try placing only one knee on an elbow.*

(continued)

Learning experiences	Teaching tips
Challenge: Balance on shoulders, back of head, and upper arms. Stretch your legs above your head as high as you comfortably can. Slowly curl your legs and body, extend one arm to the side on the floor, tuck your chin, and turn your head toward the opposite arm as you transition to a balance of your choice using a backward safety shoulder roll.	*Students not ready for this challenge can choose to curl and roll sideways.*
Challenge: Explore balances on different bases of support, using narrow or curling rolling actions to transfer out of and into new balances. Make sure that your transitions flow well from one balance to the roll and then to the new balance. Always follow the safety rules for inverted balances.	*List on the whiteboard or screen all the body parts that can serve as bases of support for balances.*

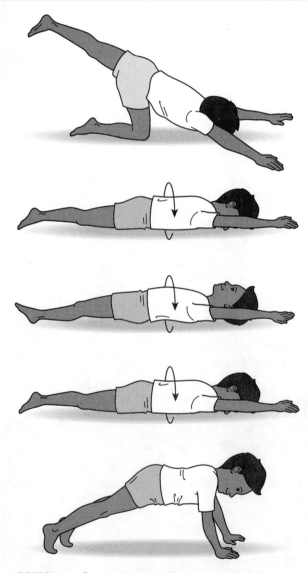

FIGURE 6.11   Sample inverted balance, roll, balance.

WEIGHT TRANSFERENCE WITH LEVELS AND SHAPES

In previous work, students learned to balance at low, medium, and high levels. They also explored wide, narrow, curled, twisted, symmetrical, and nonsymmetrical body shapes. The previous learning experiences focused on stretching, twisting, curling, and rolling as options for weight transfers between balances. Next in the progression is combining the balances at different levels and shapes with the weight transfer actions. The students will discover that connecting the level or shape of a balance to a specific weight transfer action will result in a much smoother transition into another balance. Later, students will create sequences wherein these new discoveries will aid their decision making. After a quick review of balancing in different levels and body shapes, students are ready to transfer from one balance to another, from one level to another, and from one body shape to another. The exploration will include the selection of effective transitioning actions.

Transfers Between Balances, Different Levels and Shapes

Cognitive: The choice of weight transfer between balances from one level to another or from one body shape to another requires selections that will result in smooth transitions.

Skills: Use twisting, stretching, curling, and rolling actions to transfer between balances at all three levels and in all body shapes.

Criteria: Quality smooth transitions to make connections between balances.

Safety: Personal space, awareness of others, use of safety protocol for inverted balances.

Equipment and organization: Scattered individual mats or enough large mats for children to work safely.

LOW LEVEL, SHAPES AND TRANSFERS

Learning experiences	Teaching tips
You are going to explore transferring between balances that are at different levels and in different body shapes. Start with a balance on your favorite bases of support at a low level. Using either a stretching, twisting, or curling action, transfer to a new balance with different bases of support, still at low level. Remember to hold the balance still for three to five seconds and then transition slowly into the new balance.	*Reinforce having extended personal space for safe transfers.*
Balance on your back at a low level with arms and legs stretched, creating a narrow body shape. Lower the arms and legs to the mat, maintain the narrow shape, and roll sideways to a new low-level balance. Remember that the narrow roll requires tight muscles and leading with the hips.	

(continued)

Learning experiences	Teaching tips
Balance on two feet and two hands at a low level in a narrow body shape. Slowly lower the body to the mat, balancing on your stomach and extending free body parts into a narrow shape. Keeping the narrow shape, roll sideways into a new balance with different bases of support.	*Provide feedback on quality balances and rolls.*
Repeat this balance, balance, roll, balance combination and concentrate on tight muscles, alignment, and extensions for your balances. Focus on maintaining tight muscles, extension, and alignment as you lead with your hips rolling sideways. Show good body control by making all your balances and transitions the best they can be.	
Balance on your seat in a curled shape. Rock backward and balance on your back while maintaining the curled shape. Tuck your chin, knees, and arms to chest and roll sideways into a different low-level balance.	
Explore different bases of support and body shapes at a low level, connecting each with a smooth weight transfer—stretching, twisting, curling, or rolling.	

MEDIUM LEVEL, SHAPES AND TRANSFERS

Learning experiences	Teaching tips
Balance on your favorite base of support at a medium level. Using either a stretching, twisting, or curling action, transfer to a new balance with different bases of support, still at medium level. Remember to hold the balance still for three to five seconds; then transition slowly into the new balance.	*Reinforce having extended personal space for safe transfers.*
Balance on two knees and one hand at a medium level. Extend the free hand in medium level. After three to five seconds, move the free hand under and beyond the body.	*Provide feedback on quality balances and rolls.*
As you twist, lower your shoulder, curl, and roll over your shoulder, ending in a balance with your seat and one foot as the base of support.	
Repeat the balance, roll, balance sequence with a focus on quality balances—tight muscles and good extensions of free body parts. Remember to keep chin on chest and stay round through your safety shoulder roll.	
Control your speed as you transfer into the second balance. If you are not comfortable with the safety shoulder roll, you may use the curled roll sideways.	

Learning experiences	Teaching tips
Balance on two hands and one foot at a medium level in a curled body shape. Slowly lower your body and transition using a curled sideways roll or a safety shoulder roll. End with a balance on two hands and one foot at a medium level in a wide body shape. Extend the free leg.	
Explore different bases of support and body shapes at medium level, connecting each with a smooth weight transfer—stretching, twisting, curling, or rolling. Remember to lower your body gently if you use rolling as a transfer.	

HIGH LEVEL, SHAPES AND TRANSFERS

Learning experiences	Teaching tips
Balance on one foot, extending arms to a high level and a narrow shape.	*Reinforce having extended personal space for transfers.*
Stretch your arms forward and downward in a wide shape while extending your free leg to counterbalance.	*Slowly lead students through the steps of this learning experience.*
Lower and curl your body until your hands are touching the mat. Your new base of support is two hands and one foot.	
Stretch one arm under your body as you twist and curl your body, tucking your chin and rolling over your open shoulder.	
Repeat this action and transition into a new balance and shape of your choice after the safety shoulder roll.	
Balance on one foot in a twisted body shape with one hand at a high level. Using a twisting action followed by a stretching action, move from a twisted body shape to a wide body shape, balancing on the other foot.	
Explore different bases of support and different shapes at a high level, connecting each with a smooth weight transfer—stretching, twisting, curling, or rolling. Remember that the entire body does not have to be a high level, just body parts—one hand, two hands, one foot, two feet, one elbow, or the head. Make sure you can hold your balance for three to five seconds.	

USING TRANSFERS TO CHANGE LEVEL OF BALANCES

Learning experiences	Teaching tips
Balance at a high level, transfer smoothly and slowly to a new balance at medium level, hold three to five seconds, and then transfer to a new balance at low level.	*Reinforce having extended personal space for safe transfers.*
Change your base of support for each balance and remember to use the stretching, twisting, curling, or rolling transfer actions. Were you able to make smooth transitions, without hesitation, as you moved from one balance to the next?	
Repeat your balance, transfer, and change of levels, focusing on selecting balances and transfer actions that allow your transition to move smoothly from one to the next. The match of balance and transfer is the key.	*Focus on quality transitions. Some students will need help selecting transfers that match balances.*
Explore the same balances in reverse, as if you are rewinding. Start low, transition to medium, and end at high level. You may not be able to use the same transfer actions. If not, change balances or transfers as needed for a smooth transition. The match for a smooth transition is the goal.	

USING TRANSFERS TO CHANGE SHAPES OF BALANCES

Learning experiences	Teaching tips
Balance on your chosen base of support with a wide body shape; free body parts should extend away from the body. Was your balance at high, medium, or low level?	*Reinforce having extended personal space for safe transfers.*
Without changing the level of the first balance, transition into a narrow shape on different bases of support. Concentrate on the smoothness as you transfer to the new base of support and to the new shape.	
Create a balance in a twisted shape at a different level. Without changing levels, transfer to a different base of support with a curled shape balance. Were you able to have different bases of support for each of the shapes?	*Make sure that students are performing gymnastic balances and not simply demonstrating the body shapes.*
Repeat the combinations from the previous two learning experiences, concentrating on making smooth transitions between the balances.	

Learning experiences	Teaching tips
Explore a combination of two balances, each with a different base of support and a different body shape, connected by a weight transfer (stretching, twisting, curling, rolling).	*Focus on quality transitions. Some students will need help selecting transfers to match balances.*
What weight transfer worked best to link your balances for a smooth transition?	*Call on a few students to share.*
Challenge: Create a series of four balances, each with a different body shape. Use at least two levels and at least two transfer actions (stretching, twisting, curling, or rolling). The weight transfers between the balances may determine the order of the shapes. Practice until you have four body shape balances and smooth transfers between them. Each balance should flow into the next. Strive for quality balances with tight muscles and good extensions. Try different balances and transfers until you think they are your best. Take your time and make good decisions.	*Emphasize safety and personal skill levels. List the following on a whiteboard or screen: low, medium, high levels; wide, narrow, curled, and twisted shapes; weight transfer actions of stretching, twisting, curling, and rolling.*
In a group of three, show your series of balances. While one person performs, one assesses for the use of all four body shapes; the third person in your group watches to be sure that two levels or more are used. I will observe for smooth transitions. Rotate positions until each of you has shown your balances, each has assessed shapes, and each has assessed levels. Give each other cues or advice for making the demonstration of balances even better.	*Place students in groups of three for this peer assessment. Make sure they know what their roles are and when to rotate roles.*

USING TRANSFERS TO CHANGE SYMMETRICAL AND NONSYMMETRICAL BALANCES

Learning experiences	Teaching tips
Balance in a symmetrical shape at a medium level. Remember that both sides of your body must be the same. Keep one side of your body as is and slowly stretch, curl, or twist one or more body parts on the other side in any direction, creating a nonsymmetrical balance.	*Reinforce having extended personal space for transfers.*
Balance in a nonsymmetrical shape at a low level. Roll sideways in a narrow body shape ending in a symmetrical balance. Repeat the nonsymmetrical body shape at a low level and roll sideways in a curled shape into a different symmetrical balance.	
Explore symmetrical and nonsymmetrical balances, using stretching, twisting, curling, or rolling actions as the transition to change the symmetry and end in a different balance.	*Focus on quality transitions. Some students will need help selecting transfers to match balances.*

WEIGHT TRANSFERENCE USING IN-FLIGHT ACTIONS

When the body is momentarily airborne, the actions are considered in-flight. Weight transfers using in-flight actions include locomotors, jumping, and feet-hands-feet travel wherein feet and hands alternately and briefly support the rest of the body. The shapes and actions created while a person is in the air are an important part of educational gymnastics and include the previously learned body shapes, turns, and stretching, twisting, and curling actions.

In its simplest form, weight transfer is locomotion (walking, hopping, running, galloping, skipping, etc.). Children typically explore these skills in preschool. Physical education teachers refine locomotors as means of travel, beginning in kindergarten. By the end of grade 2, children should be able to perform the mature pattern of locomotor skills, except for leaping (SHAPE America 2014). The movement concepts of pathways and directions enhance the travel actions. The locomotor skills of hopping, jumping, galloping, skipping, sliding sideways, and running when performed correctly all have brief moments when both feet are off the ground. Refinement of these skills with a focus on critical elements is prerequisite to learning experiences when locomotors are used as weight transfers to connect balances. Later, locomotors will be used as an approach to begin an individual or partner sequence and to approach equipment.

Jumping is a skill that young children love to explore. When a toddler explores ways to move, jumping off a low item such as a bottom step brings them joy. They also explore other ways to jump but rarely do they achieve height or distance. They simply jump for the sensation of leaving the ground. Just as with locomotors, starting in kindergarten, physical education teachers provide learning experiences that lead to the mature patterns of jumping and landing. Jumping consists of three phases: takeoff, flight, and landing, and all three phases must be taught emphasizing the critical elements. The fundamental jumping and landing patterns include two feet to two feet, one foot to two feet, one foot to the same foot (hop), one foot to the opposite foot (leap), and two feet to one foot. These five patterns with an emphasis on the three phases are prerequisite to building the skills and confidence needed for flight experiences in educational gymnastics. Jumping in educational gymnastics includes an emphasis on the in-flight actions of stretching, twisting, turning, and creating body shapes. The in-flight actions will also be used as transfers into and out of balances. Later, in chapter 7, these experiences are combined with jumping on or off gymnastics equipment. Landing is always emphasized for safety and for preparation for the next balance or action.

Transferring weight from feet to hands is a skill that children enjoy, but children must have both cognitive and performance understanding of the safety factors involved in practice of the skill. A child must also have the prerequisite strength and the self-responsibility not to attempt actions beyond their individual ability. The transfer of weight from feet to hands results in a momentary airborne phase as well as a brief balance of weight on hands. The transfer of weight from feet to hands to feet in a new location for travel and transfers into and out of balances are components of educational gymnastics. Just as in jumping, the in-flight actions of stretching, twisting, turning, and creating body shapes can be explored. Handstands and walking on hands are reserved for after-school gymnastics programs.

 Taking weight on hands leads quickly to arm and shoulder fatigue. The in-flight weight transfer experiences of jumping and feet-hands-feet actions are best developed with distributed practice over several lessons (see chapter 3).

Locomotors and Other Actions With Balances

Cognitive: Movement actions add variety to locomotor travel. Balances can be connected with locomotor travel. Stretching, twisting, and curling actions of the body or body parts enhance the travel and transfers.

Skills: Connecting balances with locomotors.

Criteria: Stillness in balances, smooth transitions, a variety of in-flight actions.

Safety: Space awareness of others when traveling, use of safe balances and in-flight actions that do not require mats.

Equipment and organization: No equipment. Use of personal and general space as indicated.

EXPLORING DIFFERENT MOVEMENTS WITH LOCOMOTORS

Learning experiences	Teaching tips
You have used locomotor skills in a variety of ways since kindergarten. Today you are going to add a little more height to your movement and include a few actions you have been using in gymnastics. Start in your personal space and remember that as you travel in general space, you need to be aware of the actions of others. As always, try to be unique in your choices. I am looking for controlled and purposeful actions, not silly movements.	*Remove mats from the teaching space.* *Allow about a minute for each of the next few learning experiences. Encourage variety and emphasize safety.*
Walk in general space raising your legs high. Feel free to bend your knees as if marching. Stretch, kick, or create your own movement making sure to maintain your balance. Add your own unique arm movements. Explore different movements until you hear the signal to stop.	
Skip using your arms and legs to help you skip high. Stretch your arms out to medium level or up to high level. Explore different movements until you hear the signal to stop.	
Gallop with your legs transferring from a narrow to a wide shape. Make your arms do the same or keep them either narrow or wide. Explore different movements until you hear the signal to stop.	
Slide sideways repeating what you did with the gallop. Try to push off your feet and get high in the air. Curl your spine slightly, bend your knees, and slide at a medium level. Explore different movements until you hear the signal to stop.	
Select your favorite from today or perhaps another you want to create. When your group is called, travel in general space while others watch your unique actions. Be careful not to travel close to others.	*Divide the class into small groups of four to six. Students perform as individuals but travel in small groups in general space. Call one group at a time. All other students remain in personal space.*

COMBINING LOCOMOTORS WITH BALANCES

Learning experiences	Teaching tips
In personal space, balance on your chosen base of support. Count to yourself for three to five seconds of stillness and then travel a short distance with your chosen locomotor. Stop and balance with a base of support different from your first balance.	*Students balance in personal space and then move only a short distance into general space. Emphasize safety by requesting that children travel into open space.*
I noticed that most of you stood up from your first balance, traveled, stopped, and then formed a balance. When you use locomotors for transitions between balances, you must think like you did with our other transfers between balances. This time, repeat your first balance; hold for three to five seconds; slowly move into position to travel by using stretching, twisting, and curling actions; travel a short distance away; stop; and slowly transition into that second balance.	
Explore different balances and different locomotors. Balance, travel, balance. As you choose the best balances, think about the transfers for smooth transitions changing to or from a locomotor travel. Think about the level, body shape, and base of support used to determine which transfer action is needed and which locomotor is the best choice.	*Emphasize the smooth transition from the locomotor action into the second balance—level and bases of support for balance.*
Challenge: You are going to create a combination of three balances with two different locomotors to connect them. Your balances must have different bases of support and at least two levels. Practice for smooth actions from your beginning balance to travel, to next balance and travel, to ending balance. Select good transitional movements from balances into locomotors and from locomotors into balances. Remember that you are sharing space with others.	
Let's allow others to see what you have created.	*Divide the class into small groups of four to six. Students perform as individuals but travel in small groups in general space. Call one group at a time. All other students remain in personal space.*

Jumping High With Turns and Shapes, Combining Balances

Cognitive: Turns and body shapes are made at the highest point of the jump and must end in a safe balanced landing.

Skills: Connection of balances with jumps that involve different takeoffs, in-flight actions, and landings.

Criteria: Stillness in balances, smooth transitions, a variety of in-flight actions, safe landings.

Safety: Space awareness of others when traveling, use of safe balances and in-flight actions that do not require mats. Safe, balanced landings.

Equipment and organization: No equipment. Use of personal and general space as indicated.

REVIEW OF JUMPING FROM TWO FEET TO TWO FEET AND ONE FOOT TO TWO FEET

Learning experiences	Teaching tips
We are going to start with a review of the two jumps used most in gymnastics. In your personal space, jump as high as you can starting on two feet and landing balanced on two feet. I noticed several of you remembered to start with bent knees and arms back, you extended your arms up as you jumped and then ended with a good, squashed landing with knees bent. Jump again as I observe for bent knees and arms back, extensions, and squash landings.	*Check for personal space extended to allow safe jumping and landing.*
Repeat the jump from two feet to two feet but this time go high and forward. Don't jump as far as you can; just make sure it is high and forward, just out of your personal space. Remember that others are also jumping.	
Now, take three steps backward. Start with a slow run, jump off one foot, and land on two feet. Keep your head up and eyes forward. Make a balanced landing.	

SHAPES IN THE AIR: WIDE, NARROW, CURLED

Learning experiences	Teaching tips
Now you are going to add shapes in the air to your jumps. Starting with your feet shoulder-width apart, jump from two feet to two feet. When you are at your highest, make a wide shape with your arms and legs. Bring your feet back to shoulder-width apart and bend knees for the landing.	*Check for personal space extended to allow safe jumping and landing.* *See figure 6.12.*
Repeat with a narrow shape. Stretch your arms and legs when at the highest point of your jump. Remember to have feet shoulder-width apart and bend knees for a balanced landing.	
The next one is a little more difficult. At the highest part of your jump, make a curled shape for just a second before coming out of the curl to land safely on your feet. You do not have to curl your whole body. Keeping your head up and eyes looking forward helps with your safe landing.	
Repeat each of the three shapes with the one foot to two feet jumping action. Remember to give yourself a couple of steps to run into this jump. Continue to practice focusing on good shapes and safe landings. Be aware of others practicing around you.	

FIGURE 6.12   Sample shapes in flight.

SHAPES IN THE AIR: SYMMETRICAL AND NONSYMMETRICAL

Learning experiences	Teaching tips
Now you are going to explore symmetrical and nonsymmetrical shapes. We will use jumps from two feet to two feet and from one foot to two feet. Without making any shapes in the air, which of the two jumps is already symmetrical and which one is nonsymmetrical? Discuss with someone near you. If you answered two feet to two feet is symmetrical and one foot to two feet is nonsymmetrical, you are correct.	*Review symmetrical and nonsymmetrical shapes.* *See figure 6.13.*
Return to your personal space and try a two feet to two feet jump and at your highest point, make a symmetrical shape with arms and legs. Jump again and alter one arm and one leg in midair to make it nonsymmetrical. Always return to feet shoulder-width apart for a balanced landing.	*Check for personal space extended to allow safe jumping and landing.*
Try a one foot to two feet jump and at the highest point, make a nonsymmetrical shape with arms and legs. Remember to give yourself a couple of steps to run into this jump. Jump again and make a symmetrical shape when in the air.	*Observe for safe landings and reinforce as needed.*

FIGURE 6.13   Sample symmetrical and nonsymmetrical jumps in flight.

JUMPS AND TURNS

Learning experiences	Teaching tips
Next, you are going to do jump turns. Begin with two feet to two feet jumps. As you take off, begin a twisting or pivoting action. Your arms can help with the rotation. The push-off with your legs and the twisting action must happen together. Try a quarter turn, jumping clockwise and landing facing the wall to your right. Then repeat, jump and turn counterclockwise facing the direction you started.	*Check for personal space extended to allow safe jumping and landing.*
Repeat with a half turn, landing facing the wall behind you. Jump with a twist, trying both clockwise and counterclockwise turns.	
Last, choose clockwise or counterclockwise and see if you can rotate three-quarters of the way around and still land safely balanced.	
Try the quarter and half turns both clockwise and counterclockwise, this time using a one foot to two feet takeoff. Remember that the push-off with your one leg and twisting action must happen together. Remember to give yourself a couple of steps to run into this jump. Use your free leg to help your arms with the rotation. If you successfully land on two feet, try the three-quarters turn. You may choose to practice the half turn if you wish.	

JUMPS AND BALANCES

Learning experiences	Teaching tips
It is time to put the jumps and balances together. Balance on your choice of a base of support. Hold it for three to five seconds. Using a transitional move, slowly stretch, twist, or curl into a position to jump two feet to two feet, land, and then transition into a balance on a different base of support. Make safe decisions because we are not using mats.	*Check for personal space extended to allow safe jumping and landing.*
Balance on a different base of support, transition with a one foot to two feet jump, and end with a different balance.	
Explore different bases of support at different levels and in different body shapes that you can connect with a variety of jumps. Explore body shapes and turns in your jumps. Remember to use smooth transitional movements to connect your balances to your jumps.	
Select one of your favorite balance, jump, balance combinations. Practice a few minutes. In a group of three, share your favorite.	*Form students into groups of three to share combinations. If time allows, encourage them to try the ones created by others in their group.*

Transferring Weight Feet-Hands-Feet

Cognitive: Transferring weight from feet to hands and back to feet makes a person momentarily airborne. Twisting and stretching actions aid in placing the feet and hands in different positions.

Skills: Transfer of weight from feet to hands for momentary balance (one to two seconds) on hands only. Transfer weight feet-hands-feet using twisting actions to place feet in new locations. Transfer weight feet-hands-feet using stretching actions to place feet in new locations.

Criteria: Push off feet, push evenly with arms, position hands to help with the rotation, and make smooth transitions between balances.

Safety: If balance is lost when inverted, twist body to return to feet or lower the body, tuck chin, and do a safety shoulder roll. Take turns on mats. Extra personal space for practice. Short duration only on hands to avoid muscle fatigue and reduce chance of injury.

Equipment and organization: Enough large mats for children to work safely or a grass area.

🔺 **Make sure mats are heavy enough not to slide. If the mat sliding is a concern, have a child stand at the opposite end to secure the mat.**

TAKING WEIGHT ON HANDS MOMENTARILY

Learning experiences	Teaching tips
Today you are going to explore transferring weight momentarily from feet, to hands, to feet. Some of you may be able to do handstands, but that is not our focus.	*Use as an introduction to these learning experiences.* *Handstand is an advanced balance skill. Weight is placed on hands only momentarily for weight transfers.* *See figure 6.14.*
In your personal space away from the mats, balance on two hands and two feet with hips raised, facing the floor. Travel on two hands and two feet a short distance from your personal space. Balance on two hands and one foot, holding for three to five seconds. Travel on two hands and one foot back to your starting place. Repeat and keep your head up to watch where you are going. Travel around, not over, the mats. As you were traveling you were momentarily moving your weight from feet to hands.	*Check for personal space extended to allow for safe landing. If mats are in place, emphasize they are not used yet.*
You are now ready to work using the mats. Lower your body, placing your hands on the mat. Starting in a curled shape, push with your hands and feet, bringing your feet just off the floor. Try it again, bringing your feet to a medium level and back down. Continue to explore, kicking up your feet and taking weight on your hands. **Always try to return safely to your feet. You may have to come back down in the same place or twist your body so that you can safely land on your feet. If you should accidently kick so far that you lose your balance, just like in our inverted balances, tuck your chin, curl your spine, and roll safely over your shoulder.**	*If mats are long enough, two students may work safely at the same time. If not, require students to take turns.* *Review safety rolls if needed.*
Challenge: Place your hands on the mat again and this time place your feet in a lunge position. Kick one leg followed quickly by the other. Explore which leg you like in front. Come down in the same place you started on one foot, the other foot, or both feet. Continue practicing, each time trying to kick your legs higher.	*Demonstrate hands on mat and the lunge position. Encourage students to kick only as high as they are comfortable.* *See figure 6.15.*
Challenge: See if you can control your body enough to make slow, quiet landings with your feet. To do this, hold the weight on your hands a little longer.	

FIGURE 6.14   Weight momentarily on hands.

FIGURE 6.15   Weight on hands, exploring height of kicking one foot upward followed by other foot.

WEIGHT TRANSFER FEET-HANDS-FEET WITH TWISTING ACTION

Learning experiences	Teaching tips
You have an idea of your comfort zone for how high to kick your legs. This time after you kick your legs, twist your body, bringing your feet down just to the right or the left. You can come down with one leg followed by the other or both at the same time. Remember to use body control for soft landings.	
You are now ready to explore taking weight on hands, twisting your body even more and having your feet come down in different places. Remember to take your legs only as high as you are comfortable. An old-fashioned clock will help as you explore how far to twist.	*Draw a large clock on the whiteboard or screen with numbers in correct places (see figure 6.16). Draw hands on the clock for 6:00. Another option is to find an electronic clock face to share on screen.*
Your feet always start at 6:00. Start with your hands stretched over your head. Lean forward, placing your hands in the same position as where the hands connect in the center of the clock while starting the lunge position with your legs. The action will be stretch, lean, lunge, kick up. Your first twist is counterclockwise to 5:00 and then clockwise to 7:00. Practice each with strong arms and soft landings. Next, go for 4:00 and 8:00. Ready for 3:00 and 9:00? As before, you can land one foot and then the other or both feet together.	*Observe for readiness. Some children may not have the prerequisite upper-body strength, and a few may simply be uncomfortable with this level of inversion.*
Challenge: Kick both legs to the same height so that they come together in the air. You can kick one leg followed by the other but pause, holding both together for one or two seconds. The height is still up to you.	*Success in this task will allow for the twisting action needed for the next challenge. For students not ready, allow them to continue with the previous learning experience.*
Challenge: When you are ready, try 10:00, 2:00, 11:00, 1:00, and even 12:00. Remember to rest between kicks; kicking is tiring. You will need to kick your highest, push strong with your arms, and increase your twist. To progress, each landing must be on your feet.	*Observe for fatigue and allow needed breaks. Observe for safe landings on feet as a prerequisite to extend this challenge.*

FIGURE 6.16   Twisting actions landing in new locations.

WEIGHT TRANSFER FEET-HANDS-FEET WITH WHEEL ACTION

Learning experiences	Teaching tips

The last challenge is to go from 6:00 to 12:00 but with more of a wheel action. Yes, this is like a cartwheel, but it does not have to be a perfect cartwheel.

Start in your stretched arms and lunge position, or you may feel more comfortable with your shoulder toward the mat. Momentarily take your weight on your back leg. Stretch forward, keeping arms extended as you shift your weight to your front foot, followed by one hand, other hand, one foot, other foot. The hands touch and push in the center of the clock one after the other, and your feet will land on the opposite side one after the other.

Demonstrate the two options for starting position as you talk through the learning experience.

- Think stretch, lean, lunge, hand, hand, foot, foot.
- Explore to see if you like to lead with your right side or your left side.

You can land at 10:00, 11:00, 12:00, 1:00, or 2:00. As before, the height of your legs is up to you.

Challenge: Keep trying to stretch your legs as high as you are comfortable traveling in a straight pathway. Use tight muscles throughout, stretch your legs, and align your hips over your shoulders and feet over your hips. This alignment will make your rotation smoother, and your landing will be closer to 12:00. As with all our gymnastics, explore within your comfort zone.

Attempt stretching action only when students have prerequisite skill of holding weight on hands for a minimum of two seconds.

Weight transfer feet-hands-feet with wheeling action.

COMBINE BALANCES AND FEET-HANDS-FEET TRANSFERS

Learning experiences	Teaching tips
You will now combine balances with the transfer of feet to hands to feet, connecting balances and transfers with weight on hands. Choose a favorite balance at medium level; hold three to five seconds and then transfer weight from feet to hands to feet, transitioning into a balance on a different base of support. Remember that you may need to stretch, twist, or curl out of your balance into a position to use the feet-hands-feet transfer.	
Explore other balance, transfer feet-hands-feet actions, balance combinations. Think about working at high, medium, and low levels.	*Some students will need help selecting balances that will transfer with feet-hands-feet.*

🚧 **Remember to be safe sharing mats and taking weight on hands.**

EDUCATIONAL GYMNASTICS SEQUENCES

Educational gymnastics sequences are a series of balances and actions that fit logically together. They are opportunities for students to demonstrate skills, cognitive understanding, and uniqueness. Sequences can be used as a culminating experience and as an assessment, both formative and summative.

Creating Individual Sequences

In previous learning experiences, students have demonstrated informal sequences. Students were asked to combine balances through weight transfer actions: stretching, twisting, curling, rolling, locomotors, jumping, and feet-hands-feet actions. These were included for students to learn to link skills and served as a foundation for more complex sequences. Students now have a large repertoire of skills and experience linking actions and balances. They are ready to begin simple to complex sequences.

A sequence consists of three parts: a beginning, middle, and ending, much like a story. The beginning consists of a shape or balance that will facilitate the first action. It should clearly say, "I am ready to begin." It may be followed by a travel, a weight transfer action, or a simple stretching, twisting, or curling transition into a balance. The middle is the combination of balances and weight transfers (including stretching, twisting, curling, and rolling actions as well as locomotion, jumping with turns and shapes, and feet-hand-feet actions) that make up the sequence. The ending is another shape, position, or balance. The last action should facilitate the ending. Many children enjoy using the ending "Ta-da," standing with arms extended to a high level with arms, shoulders, hips, and feet aligned. The choice of shape, position, or balance should say, "I am finished."

The teacher initiates the sequence by providing the specific requirements that should be included. As students gain experience, the teacher may encourage students to go beyond the given expectations. At all times the performance criteria should include balances held in stillness for three to five seconds and smooth, linking weight transfers. The requirements of the sequence should be posted on a whiteboard or screen; they can also be given to students and serve as a checklist as students are working. Students will need paper and pencil to record their sequences. The handout, with requirements and instruction for completion, becomes the sequence assignment sheet (see Sequence Assignment in appendix).

Sequence assignments begin with the exploring and selecting phase of creating the middle part of sequences. Later, the beginning and the ending will be added. This exploring and selecting process should not be rushed. It includes thought, action, and trial and error. Some children spend time thinking, whereas others begin moving immediately. Some children want to finish quickly and will need encouragement to explore other options. Others need reminders to begin. You will need to move about and give feedback or ask questions that help the students with their decision making. Examples beyond positive feedback include the following:

- "Have you tried other ways so that you can determine which works best?"

- "Remember that your transitions need to be intentional and not just happen. Think about each one."

- "Have you tried slowing down (or speeding up) that transitional move? Adjusting your momentum may help you move into that next balance or action."

- "I see (insert criteria). Well done! Have you included the following (insert criteria)?"

The next phase is putting the final touches on the sequence. The purpose is to refine it, making it the best it can be. Organization and often reorganization occur here. Students are now ready to add the beginning and ending shapes. This phase may not be as time consuming as the previous one, but it should not be rushed. Children need focused practice time, as the teacher's questions shift to specifics related to smooth, transitional moves that can make or break the organization of the sequence.

- "Is each balance or action related to the next?"
- "Are you holding all balances for three to five seconds with smooth and controlled transitional movements that move into the next action or balance?"

Students struggle with continuity, the most important part of the sequence. They find it hard to see that the ending of a previous action must flow smoothly into the beginning of the next movement or balance. Here is where examples and nonexamples demonstrated by the teacher can be helpful. Sometimes the overexaggerating demonstration of a balance, transfer, balance with no flow sends the message and provides a few laughs. The match between balances and the transfer out of the balances is the most critical piece for safety and for smoothness. Remind students to think ahead by landing in a position that leads easily to the next action.

If cameras or tablets are available, have students work in partners and record, allowing them to view their sequence and make final refinements. Working in pairs observing someone else live or using a recording and giving helpful hints is also beneficial. Following peer feedback, students are ready to make any refinements to their sequences (final edits on their assignment sheet) and practice the sequence until they memorize it.

When students are ready to show their sequences, it is not recommended that they perform for the entire class. Some students will be uncomfortable, and the presentations are time consuming. Placing students with a partner or in small groups works well. Peers can be given specific observation points (requirements of the sequence) or just observe. If the sequence is to be used as a teacher assessment, assess while others are still practicing or video-record and assess later. In both peer and teacher observations, quality and evidence of meeting the sequence requirements are goals of the sequences (see chapter 8).

The learning experiences that follow begin with a review of linking balances. Then, using the process explained earlier, guide the students through the creation and performance of their unique sequence. The one provided here is an example. Alter the requirements of the sequence based on individual skill development and comfort in sequence development. Anticipate that sequences will take more than one class period.

Individual Sequences in Action

Cognitive: An understanding of the process and requirements of the sequence.

Skills: Create and perform a sequence that meets the criteria supplied by the teacher.

Criteria: Provided in the requirements by the teacher. Balances held for three to five seconds; smooth, flowing transitions; variety; and creativity.

Safety: Use space and mats safely. Take turns on the mat if required. When not on the mat, practice that can safely be done on the floor or grass.

Equipment and organization: Enough large mats for children to work safely with a partner.

REVIEW OF BALANCE AND WEIGHT TRANSFER COMBINATIONS

Learning experiences	Teaching tips

You are ready to combine all you have learned about balances and weight transfers into your personal gymnastics sequence. Let's review a few combinations first.

Review safety for sharing mats. You may wish to control taking turns by announcing partner A and the task and then repeat for partner B.

Choose your favorite balances in the combinations that I name and focus on slow, smooth, controlled, and flowing transitional moves into a different balance. All balances must be held still for three to five seconds with tight muscles, and, where appropriate, extensions of free body parts and alignment. Explore to determine the combination that matches transfer to balance. If time allows, try another one with the same requirements. Do not forget to add levels and shapes and make your combinations unique.

- Balance, stretch into a new balance.
- Balance, twist into a new balance.
- Balance, curl and roll into a new balance.
- Balance, travel, balance.
- Balance, jump, land, balance.
- Balance, jump, land, roll sideways or over the shoulder, balance.
- Travel, balance, feet-hands-feet action, balance.

Challenge: Choose your favorite three balances, using different combinations of body parts as bases of support. Select an action to transfer out of each and into a new balance: balance #1, transfer, balance #2, transfer, balance #3. Practice to determine what is the best order of the balances and what transfer action leads smoothly out of and into the next balance. Remember to hold each balance for three to five seconds before you transfer.

Determine how partners will take turns for this task. The partner waiting can provide feedback on smooth transitions.

See figure 6.17.

FIGURE 6.17   Example combination three balances and two transfers.

INDIVIDUAL SEQUENCE CREATION AND PERFORMANCE

Learning experiences	Teaching tips

You are now ready to create and perform a complete gymnastics sequence. The requirements of the sequence are written on the whiteboard (or screen) and are on your assignment sheet. You can see that your sequence includes a beginning shape, a middle, and an ending shape to your sequence. You are going to start with the middle.

- Your sequence must have four different balances, one of which must be inverted (head lower than most of the body), three different transitional moves, of which one must be in-flight, a change in levels, and at least two body shapes. The body shapes can be in the balances or in the transitional moves. Remember that you must hold all balances for three to five seconds, show good muscular tension and alignment, and be controlled and smooth in your transitional actions.

- Now, you are ready to add a beginning and ending shape. The beginning shape should show, "I am ready to begin," and easily transition into the first part of your sequence. The ending shape should flow out of your last balance or action. It should say, "I am finished." You can use the "Ta-da" pose if it fits with your sequence. Work for a while and continue to make your sequence the best it can be by having all parts link smoothly together.

When your sequence is complete and memorized, you are ready to show it to a friend who will watch and give any cues for refinement. They will also check your written work for completion. Remember to do the same for the person who helped you.

Distribute the appendix handout (Sequence Assignment) and pencils in an efficient manner.

Determine how partners will take turns for this task. The partner waiting can provide feedback on smooth transitions.

After reading the introduction to this section, guide the students through the process of exploring, selecting, refining, and sharing their sequences. Remember that the sequence process is time consuming and will take more than one class period. Use of individual student portfolios or class folders provides the organization needed from one class meeting to the next.

Creating Partner Sequences

Partner sequences involve the same process as individual sequences except that more time needs to be allowed for communicating and reaching agreements. Partners need to cooperate and understand each other's abilities. Timing is the most difficult part to achieve.

Two common partner actions for sequences are copying and matching ideas or actions. Copying is like follow the leader except one partner completes the action before the other partner goes. The second partner may not have the skill to copy exactly but still must include the idea of the task. For example, partners travel across the mat in a feet-hands-feet action. One person may do a cartwheel with good extensions and control. The partner may stay at a medium level but still meet the same criteria. Matching is doing the same action in unison. The positions may be side by side facing the same direction, side by side facing the opposite direction, or facing each other passing on the side. As before, both partners should follow the idea of the movement, but may not be identical in skill level. Many students like to include partner counterbalances. Previous counterbalance experiences using counter-tension and counter-resistance should be reviewed. They may be used within the sequence as a meet and part relationship or as beginning or ending shapes. Other options are shown in the appendix at the end of chapter 5.

Partner Sequences in Action

Cognitive: An understanding of the process and requirements of the sequence. The need for communication and decision making.

Skills: Create and perform a partner sequence that meets the criteria supplied by the teacher.

Criteria: Balances held for three to five seconds, smooth and flowing transitions, matching or near matching movements, variety, and creativity.

Safety: Use space and mats safely.

Equipment and organization: Enough large mats for children to work safely with a partner.

PARTNER RELATIONSHIPS

Learning experiences	Teaching tips
Previously you created and performed your own sequences. Today you are going to begin working on a partner sequence. Find a partner and stand one behind the other.	*Partners should be able to work well together; best friends are not always the best partners for sequences. Depending on the type of sequence, such as matching or copying, partners of similar skill may be best.*
The first learning experiences will be follow-the-leader copycat. I will give you some information, and you add creativity. If the leader does a move that you cannot copy exactly, perform it as best you can but make it meet the requirements. You can ask your partner to repeat it if you need to see it again. After one partner leads, the other copies, and partners then change roles. Keep taking turns until I call the next one.	*Allow a few minutes of taking turns on the same task before introducing the next one in the series.*

- Travel a short distance in general space using locomotors and flight actions of your choice. Stop and let your partner copy. Be aware of others and make good, safe landings.
- Travel on the mat using a feet-hands-feet action. Stop at the other end and allow your partner to copy.
- Balance, transitional move of your choice, different balance. Hold the balances and make smooth transitions. Do not rush.

Learning experiences	Teaching tips
Next, you and your partner are going to do matching actions. These take much more communication and practice with timing. There are several possible partner relationships. My partner and I will demonstrate. You can decide if you want to be side by side facing the same direction, opposite directions, or coming toward each other and passing. You can even try a meet and part if you like. Each idea requires communication and planning.	*Demonstrate each relationship with a student partner.* *Post on a whiteboard or screen, allowing students to work at their own pace. Provide sufficient time for students to explore all the partner relationships.*

- Travel using locomotors and in-flight actions.

- Travel across the mat using feet-hands-feet actions.

- Balance, transitional action, balance. Stay with this one awhile and experiment with stretching, twisting, curling, rolling, locomotors, jumping, and hands-feet-hands transfers. Learn what your partner is most comfortable doing as well as challenges you are both up to trying. Remember to space well and move safely.

Now you and your partner are going to experiment with meeting and parting using counter-tension and counter-resistance partner balances. Spacing, timing, and communication are important for success.

- Balance side by side on your knees and feet about elbow length apart, join inside arms, extend outside arm for counterbalance, and stretch away from each other keeping arms joined as you create the counter-tension. Hold five seconds and then pull back together, curl your body, and do a curled roll sideways away from each other into a different balance.

- Using the worksheet of counterbalance options, practice the sequences of the counterbalances, transition away, and end in a new balance. Begin in a balance and transition into a partner counterbalance. Keep in mind all the transitional moves you have learned.

Hand out the chapter 5 appendix, counterbalance challenges.

PARTNER SEQUENCE CREATION AND PERFORMANCE

Learning experiences	Teaching tips
You and your partner are ready to create your partner sequence. Remember that this requires give and take as you create and select your balances and actions. The sequence must include the following as written on your second handout: • Three different balances • At least two different transitional moves • One partner counterbalance • Two of the following: locomotor travel, jump turn, jump with body shape in air, feet-hands-feet action • A beginning and ending shape	*Create a handout for partner sequences similar to the one used for individual sequences.* *Guide and question the students as you move around using similar questions from the individual sequences. When students are ready, progress to the refining stage, which may include video recordings. As with the individual sequences, allow students to share in small groups for refinement suggestions and for peer assessment.*

Summary

The experiences of combining balance and weight transfer provide optimal body control and confidence in future movement opportunities. The thrill of rolling, balancing in an inverted position, taking weight on hands, and jumping while turning or making shapes in the air are some of the fondest moments of physical education. Combining all they have learned into their personally created sequences is a proud moment for all children.

Looking ahead, the educational gymnastics progression continues in chapter 7 as students are given the opportunity to take many of the skills performed on mats and apply them to equipment available in most schools. The learning experiences include ways to get on and off equipment as well as balances and weight transfers that are possible while on the equipment. For schools fortunate enough to have regulation balance beams, appendix A in chapter 7 is devoted to applying the skills learned as well as new experiences specific to the beam.

References

SHAPE America—Society of Health and Physical Educators. 2014. *National Standards for K-12 Physical Education.* Author: Reston, VA.

Appendix

SEQUENCE ASSIGNMENT

Name:_____

Homeroom: _____

Using stick figures, sketch your sequence. Be sure to include all the following:

- Beginning shape and ending shape
- Balances: four, each with a different base of support, and at least one inverted
- Transitions: three, one connecting each balance, at least one in-flight
- Levels: two or more
- Body shapes: two or more

Practice it, memorize it, and, when ready, have a friend watch your sequence.

Draw your balances and transitional moves in order:

Draw your beginning and ending shapes:

Educational Gymnastics With Equipment

The introduction of gymnastics equipment opens a new world of learning experiences for children. Gymnastics equipment adds new dimensions to balance, transfer of weight and travel with new heights, increased bases of support, travel along, over, and under as well as on and off equipment, and configurations of equipment for their work. Suddenly, the scope of learning experiences is widened with new exploration and skill development.

Olympic-style gymnastics apparatus includes parallel bars (even and uneven bars), high balance beams, vaulting tables for travel over, and pommel horses and rings for men. Each piece of equipment is designed for specific approaches, advanced transfers and in-flight actions, and creative dismounts with advanced aerial actions of twists, turns, and flips. Traditional Olympic-style apparatus is not appropriate for educational gymnastics. Its use is reserved for highly trained gymnasts and after-school, competitive programs. The only piece of gymnastics apparatus that fits within the elementary school educational gymnastics program is the balance beam. Appendix A provides information and learning experiences for the 4-foot-high (120 cm) balance beam.

The equipment available for educational gymnastics varies by schools. Some have the budget for equipment made specifically for educational gymnastics with names such as Whittle, Southhampton Cave, and Gerstung. These items typically include climbing frames, combinations of bars, curved bridges, straight horizontal ladders, planks, and platforms. Other schools may have low balance beams and benches. For those on a limited budget, educational gymnastics equipment may consist of a variety of platforms such as benches, bottom bleachers, low stages, wooden boxes, aerobic steps, folded mats, and low sturdy tables (figure 7.1). Most elementary schools have playgrounds with bars, ladders, and platforms.

Equipment specific for educational gymnastics.
Photo courtesy of the authors.

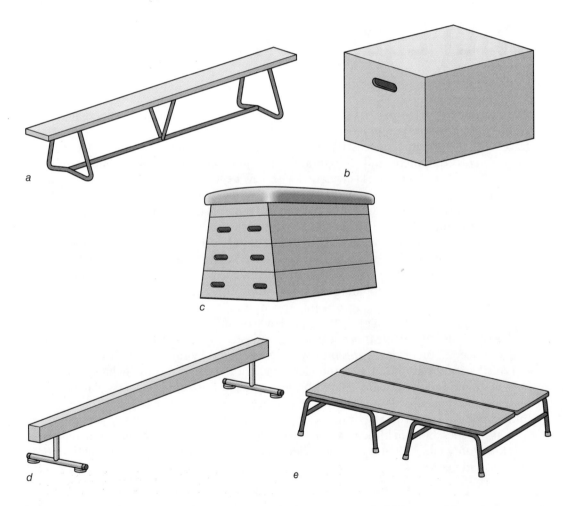

FIGURE 7.1   Example platforms for educational gymnastics include *(a)* bench, *(b)* sturdy wooden box, *(c)* adjustable vaulting box, *(d)* low balance beam, and *(e)* sturdy low table.

Although school settings differ in the types of equipment available for educational gymnastics, they all have the necessary equipment for expanded learning experiences of balance, weight transfer, and travel for children. The beauty of educational gymnastics is that the equipment does not dictate its use; instead, it offers students an environment to create their unique responses to the task presented. By not dictating the response, as with Olympic-style apparatus, the equipment is open to each child's skill level and creativity. This chapter provides learning experiences for all children, in all physical education environments. Although adaptations will be necessary based on equipment available, all physical education programs can and should provide educational gymnastics experiences on equipment. Appropriate equipment for the learning experiences will be noted throughout the chapter to assist in the selection of content.

Regardless of the type or amount of gymnastics equipment you have available for your program, mats are extremely important. Although small individual mats, and sometimes no mats, are appropriate for children working on balances and weight transfers with no equipment (chapters 5 and 6), mats are necessary for learning experiences on equipment. Sufficient mats must be available to surround the equipment as well as cover the pathways for travel to the equipment and mounts and dismounts from the equipment. Available mats often determine the equipment that can be used for educational gymnastics.

Students should not use any piece of equipment unless sufficient mats are available to ensure their safety.

Establishing a Safe Environment for Gymnastics Equipment

Safety is of paramount importance in physical education, and especially so in gymnastics. The organization of the equipment, getting on and off the equipment, the freedom for exploration, and the challenge of new balances and new ways to travel all pose issues of safety. In an environment of self-responsibility and multiple levels of skill development within each class, a safe environment is essential for all work in educational gymnastics.

Organizing Gymnastics Equipment

Educational gymnastics equipment is arranged to meet the focus of the learning experience and to provide maximum participation for the students. The equipment can be used individually or in groupings designed by the teacher to provide the best venue for the learning experience. These decisions will be based on the amount of equipment available, the quantity of mats available to be placed under equipment and for safe dismounts, and the number of students in a class. Learning experiences throughout this chapter are organized using stations as the setting for those experiences.

Stations are a common practice used in educational gymnastics to allow maximum participation on climbing frames, combinations of bars, curved bridges, horizontal ladders, benches, low beams, and platforms. We have found that an arrangement of stations

---

Homemade Gymnastics Equipment

If you are considering constructing gymnastics equipment, you must check with your school district and your school administration for their approval. We do not recommend homemade equipment for children's gymnastics.

Exploring balances on equipment.
Photo courtesy of the authors.

minimizes wait time and allows the teacher to observe all students. Initial decisions include number of stations, arrangement of equipment, number of students at each station, and a signal for safely coming off equipment for rotation to the next station. Depending on the number of stations, students may or may not achieve a full rotation to all stations in a single class period. Avoid rushing the students through the stations; exploration and creation time is critical for skill development. If the rotation to all stations requires continuing into the next class period, begin that class with a review of the focus for the lesson and have the children sit at the station where they last worked during the previous physical education class. After they are seated, they rotate to the next station, the beginning one for the day.

Although stations are a common organization for gymnastics, you may choose a different class organization for your teaching of gymnastics experiences on equipment. For example, learning experiences involving balancing on platforms or jumping and landing off equipment may use a variety of platforms (e.g., benches, bottom bleachers, vaulting boxes, steps, wooden boxes, aerobic steps, folded mats, low sturdy tables). If you have a variety of equipment available and sufficient mats to allow one piece of equipment per two students, then all are actively involved. Provide a signal after a few minutes of work to encourage students to try other equipment.

Exploration and Discovery on Gymnastics Equipment

The exploration of gymnastics equipment provides the opportunity for children to establish safe ways to travel and balance on the various pieces of equipment, as well as to develop the spatial awareness needed for self and others. Children should be introduced to the equipment and become comfortable on the equipment at an early age. Pre-K and kindergarten students enjoy exploration of the various pieces of gymnastics equipment and quickly gain respect for the equipment and the reasons for the established rules. Although adjustments may be necessary for some of the higher pieces of equipment, in general young children are free to explore and discover travel and balances on all the gymnastics equipment.

As children progress in their gymnastics learning experiences, they develop new skills of balance and weight transfer. This increase in skill development stimulates new exploration and the discovery of a higher level of balance and weight transfer. Thus, the exploration of equipment is important for all children each time the gymnastics equipment environment is set for children.

Safety on Gymnastics Equipment

The first work of children on gymnastics equipment is to establish safety—safety in travel, in balancing, in getting off equipment, and in being spatially aware of others. The first class should begin with a discussion of the rules for safe participation. All students, from the lowest to the highest grade level in the school, both new students and those returning, need to be actively engaged in this discussion. Children need to know the range of possibilities for travel and each piece of equipment and any absolute "No's" for that equipment. For example, students must never stand on top of a curved bridge, never balance on feet alone on ladders, and always face a ladder when descending it. Each teacher determines the specifics for safety in their learning environment. With equipment arranged for all children to be actively involved in the learning experience, safety and spatial awareness are critical to children's work on gymnastics equipment in physical education.

Safety protocols need to be discussed with the children before any work on gymnastics equipment. General safety rules, as well as those specific to individual pieces of equipment, need to be displayed prominently in the work area and reviewed throughout the work on equipment. If rules for safety were displayed during children's work on balances and weight transfers on mats, discuss each rule relating to the specific pieces of equipment, such as ladders, bridges, and beams.

When children were working on mats and the floor surface for balances and weight transfers, they learned to return to their feet if they were in an unsafe position. If a return to the feet was not possible, they curled the body, tucked the chin, and used a safety shoulder roll out of the balance. Depending on the gymnastics equipment on which children are working, the safety shoulder roll may not be the safe recovery. Discuss with the class safety in travel and recovery of balance for individual pieces, as well as configurations of equipment.

Basic safety rules for gymnastics equipment may include the following:

- Never touch or distract a person working in gymnastics, either on equipment or on the floor.

- Be sure you have adequate space between you and others working on the equipment to allow each person to come safely out of any balance or transfer.

- Do not copycat others in their work. Stay within your level of skill development.

- Always know your safe exit from a balance, transfer, or travel on each piece of gymnastics equipment. Remember that you may be under, on top of, or inverted on the piece of equipment.

The second major safety factor for students working on gymnastics equipment is the awareness of others and respect for their space. Students will be working at several stations within the learning area. Some will be on equipment; others will be working on the floor. Still others may be working with paper and pencil to record balances, transfers, and responses to tasks.

A teaching tip that has proved to be effective in educational gymnastics is a safety check. At any time, if you as the teacher observe an unsafe use of space or a lack of spatial awareness, signal the children to stop immediately and assume a listening position. When you say, "Safety check," students are to survey the area where they are working and adjust as needed to provide a safe amount of working space for everyone. When children learn this at an early age, it becomes a part of their personal protocol for working in gymnastics. And finally, establish the signal for any student in an unsafe position on equipment to let you as the teacher know they need help.

Mini Index for Learning Experiences

Safe Balances and Travel on Equipment...143

   Safety When Balancing and Traveling on Equipment...............................143

      Introduction to Balances and Travel..144

   Safe Landings Off Gymnastics Equipment..145

      Landing Safely...146

Balances and Weight Transfer on Equipment..147

   Balance and Transfer..147

      Balances and Transitions...148

      Levels..150

      Shapes: 4 + 2...151

      Variety and Quality in Balances and Transitions............................152

Gymnastics Equipment Mounts and Dismounts..153

   Exploration of Mounts Onto Equipment..153

      Mounting From a Stationary Position..154

      Mounting With Travel, Climbing, and Jumping Actions........................156

   Exploration of Dismounts From Equipment...156

      Balances and Transfers to Dismounts.......................................157

   Jumping Off Equipment With a Two-Foot Takeoff...................................159

      Safe Landings From New Heights...160

      Jumping With In-Flight Actions and Shapes..................................161

Sequences on Equipment...163

   Individual Sequences on Equipment Overview......................................163

   Individual Sequences in Action..163

      Creating and Performing Individual Sequences...............................164

   Partner Sequences on Equipment Overview...166

   Partner Sequences in Action...166

      Exploring Partner Options..167

      Creating and Performing Partner Sequences..................................168

SAFE BALANCES AND TRAVEL ON EQUIPMENT

With the arrangement of gymnastics equipment decided and the safety protocols established, the first learning experiences will assist students in their exploration—moving over, under, along, and through—as well as balancing and gaining confidence on the equipment. The next learning experiences will focus on safe landings. Observation of students as they explore gymnastics equipment will quickly reveal the need for focused work on safe landings. Children are traveling on body parts other than feet more than on their feet. They are traveling upside down, twisting and turning in and out of bars, and balancing on bases of support that were never possible in their previous work on mats. Often they give little thought to transferring out of the balance or terminating the travel with a return to the floor. Although unsafe landings when balancing and transferring weight on the floor can result in a bruise, unsafe landings from gymnastics equipment can result in serious injuries. Students need focused learning experiences on landing safety from the equipment after traveling, balancing, or transferring weight on the equipment.

 You may find that the teaching of the first two series of learning experiences, Safety When Balancing and Traveling on Equipment and Safe Landings Off Gymnastics Equipment, must be taught simultaneously. If needed, merge the two into one series to emphasize the importance of safety.

Safety When Balancing and Traveling on Equipment

Cognitive: Awareness of others is critical when working on gymnastics equipment. When you hear, "Safety check," stop and survey the area in which you are working for adequate space for everyone to work safely. Remember the "head plus two" rule for inverted balances on equipment if the head is a choice for one base of support.

Skills: Balance and travel safely on gymnastics equipment. Respond correctly to "Safety check."

Criteria: Demonstrate safe balances and travel on gymnastics equipment. Demonstrate awareness of safe space for others.

Safety: Sufficient space for all gymnastics stations and surrounding open space. Responsibility for self and others.

Equipment and organization: Age-appropriate (elementary school) educational gymnastics equipment with sufficient mats in place for safety. Gymnastics equipment properly positioned within the work area with adequate spacing between and around all pieces of equipment for safety.

INTRODUCTION TO BALANCES AND TRAVEL

Learning experiences	Teaching tips
Today you will begin work on gymnastics equipment—ladders, curved bridges, platforms, triangles (the pieces of equipment in the work area).	On the first day of work on gymnastics equipment, review the rules for safety for self and others. With the children seated in listening position (not on equipment), state general safety rules, as well as those specific to individual pieces of equipment. ▲ **Safety is critical when children are working on gymnastics equipment.** Name all the pieces of equipment that are in the learning area. Educational gymnastics equipment is different from Olympic apparatus; terms may be new to children.
Your work today will focus on traveling on the equipment. This travel will be different from your previous work on the mats. You can now travel over, under, along the surface; you may travel up and down, in and out of bars and ladders. You may travel forward, backward, side to side, and with turns. Explore all the ways to travel on the equipment at your station, remembering that others are also moving on the same equipment. When you hear the signal, it will be either to rotate to the next station or for a safety check. Come down safely from the equipment and sit in listening position at that station.	Divide the class into equal groups for work at each of the stations. Tell each group where to begin. They will remain at that station until you give the signal to rotate to the next station. Remind the children of the protocol for safety check. Practice of the safety check is also a good idea.
Travel forward and backward on the beam or bench, keeping the shoulders erect and eyes focused forward.	
Travel forward, do a quarter-pivot turn, and then travel sideways across the beam or bench.	
Travel forward on the beam or bench, pause, do a quarter-pivot turn, and continue your forward travel to the end of the platform.	
As you are traveling on gymnastics equipment at your station, stop and balance, maybe even using the body parts that are your base for traveling, as the bases of support for your balances.	Remind the children of stillness in balances.
Balance on a favorite base or bases of support; travel, using a change of direction to take you to a new location for a balance (ladders, bridges, beams, benches, low tables).	When children begin independent selection of bases of support, remind them of the "head plus two" rule for all balances that have the head as a base of support.
Explore traveling and balancing—traveling in different ways, balancing in ways that were not possible on the mats, such as hanging upside down by the back of the knees on the bars or twisting in and out of the rungs of the ladder and freezing in that position. ▲ **Some of you are using your head as one of your bases of support for your balances on the platforms and benches. Remember "head plus two" for all balances with the head as a base of support.**	Remind the children that anytime they are hanging upside down, they must always have a handhold. Until you assess the readiness of children for inverted balances using "head plus two" as the bases of support on equipment, establish the protocol that the student must ask your permission. Observe for safety.

Traveling across a folded mat, feet-hands-feet.

Safe Landings Off Gymnastics Equipment

Cognitive: Safe landings in gymnastics require landing on two feet, with a wide base and knees bent, alignment of body parts with hips over feet and shoulders over hips, and head erect (figure 7.2). Regardless of the type of travel, whether over, under, in and out, safe landings are always on two feet.

Skills: Safe landings from all balances, weight transfers, and travel on gymnastics equipment.

Criteria: Landing on two feet, shoulder-width apart, alignment, no loss of balance.

Safety: Personal space, awareness of others when dismounting equipment.

Equipment and organization: Educational gymnastics equipment designed for elementary school students with sufficient mats in place for safety. Gymnastics equipment properly positioned with adequate spacing between and around all pieces of equipment.

FIGURE 7.2   Safe landing.

LANDING SAFELY

Learning experiences	Teaching tips
As you were traveling, balancing, and transferring weight on the different pieces of gymnastics equipment, you were getting off the equipment in various ways. Some of you climbed down, some jumped, and others appeared in a bit of a dilemma about how to get off the equipment. The landings appeared unsafe at times, with a measure of luck keeping you from injury. As you work at stations today, your focus will be on the dismount—getting off the equipment safely.	*Begin each class with a short review of safety protocols when working on gymnastics equipment—children seated in listening position, not on equipment.*
	Praise the safe work from the previous lesson, pinpointing specific examples and highlighting any special safety concerns for this lesson.
	Introduce the proper word for getting off gymnastics equipment—the dismount.
The criteria for a safe landing are landing on two feet with feet shoulder-width apart and knees bent, alignment with hips over ankles and shoulders over hips, and eyes forward. You may raise your arms for the "Ta-da," or you may choose to extend them forward for added balance.	*Ensure that children are scattered in personal space with sufficient room for extending arms when practicing jumping and landing.*
Demonstrate that position in your personal space. Have the person beside you check for feet shoulder-width apart, knees bent, and alignment. Give your partner a high five if all is correct or offer tips for correction if needed.	
Travel onto, across, and off the equipment, focusing on safe landings to meet the criteria of landing on two feet and no loss of balance: • Travel under ladder or curved bridge; transfer with hands to continue travel or drop and land on feet. Remember to use two feet for landings. • Travel on top of curved bridge or low ladder; continue travel to climb down, transfer to hands under the bridge or ladder to continue travel, or drop and land on two feet. • Travel across bench, low beam, or plank; jump off, landing on two feet. • Travel into and out of bars on triangle, ladders, climbing frames; climb down, hang by hands, and drop to landing on two feet. • Balance, travel across platform, jump off, landing on two feet with no loss of balance.	*Divide the class into equal groups for work at the equipment stations. They will stay at that station until you give the signal to rotate to the next station.* *Remind the children that the piece of equipment may dictate how they will travel—over, under, across, in and out.* *Focus of lesson at all stations is on safe landings.*
Travel across the equipment with your favorite way to travel—forward, backward, side to side, dismounting with a safe landing. 🔺 **Remember, for all dismounts, land on two feet with no loss of balance.**	*Remind the children that regardless of the type of travel or the body parts used for the travel, landings will always be on two feet.*
Balance with your favorite base of support on the equipment. Transfer to the body parts needed for a safe dismount. The bases of support for the balance may determine the dismount.	

BALANCES AND WEIGHT TRANSFER ON EQUIPMENT

With gymnastics equipment greatly expanding the possibilities for balances on different bases of support, students are ready for guided exploration of balances and transfers into and out of balances. They have demonstrated spatial awareness for others working as well as safe landings from equipment. The balances and transfers from work on the floor or mats will serve as the foundation for the following learning experiences.

When children begin to create balances and weight transfers on gymnastics equipment at stations, they can easily forget what balances they have done and where. We have found that recording balances in the form of stick figures helps to promote variety as children move from station to station. These personal worksheets (distribute blank paper) also assist when children begin to develop sequences and recall their work at each station. See chapter 3 for suggestions on procedures for student paper and pencil recording.

Balance and Transfer

Cognitive: Balances on gymnastics equipment may be on, under, and in and out of equipment. Balances can be on different bases of support, some of which were not possible on the floor. Balances can be at different levels and in different shapes. Balances and the transfer into and out of each should be a match for smoothness.

Skills: Balance on a variety of bases of support on different pieces of gymnastics equipment. Balance at different levels and with different shapes. Smooth transitions into and out of balances.

Criteria: Stillness in balances. Smooth transfers into and out of balances. Variety in balances and in travel.

Safety: Personal space. Awareness of others. Balances and transfers that match the readiness of individual students.

Equipment and organization: Educational gymnastics equipment positioned with adequate spacing between and around all pieces of equipment for safety. Paper and pencils. Established protocol for distribution of paper and pencils to students, assigned area for written work, and placement of that work when completed for the day's assignment.

BALANCES AND TRANSITIONS

Learning experiences	Teaching tips
Today you will work again at the gymnastics stations. The focus of your work will be balances and transferring weight into and out of balances on the equipment. But before we begin let's review the safety rules for working on equipment: • Tell your neighbor one of the rules for working at gymnastics stations. • What does spatial awareness mean in gymnastics? Why is it important? • Standing in your personal space, show me the body position for a safe landing. • What does safety check mean?	*With students seated in personal space, not on equipment, begin the class with an introduction to the focus for the day, that is, balances on equipment and a review of the safety rules with questions posed and children responding.* *Have students share responses with the class.*
Today you will work again at the gymnastics stations. The focus of your work will be balances and transferring weight into and out of those balances. The first focus of your work will be bases of support. When you are working on the piece of gymnastics equipment at your station, create balances on different bases of support, remembering that you may now balance on top, under, and on the side of the equipment. Also remember that balances on top of the equipment should be balances you were able to do safely on the mats. The focus of your work is on balances on different bases of support.	*Divide the class into equal groups for the stations. Have students rotate through the stations so that they work equally at each one.* *See figure 7.3.* *Different pieces of equipment facilitate balances on different bases of support, such as ladders versus platforms. Assist children as needed with the body parts best suited as bases of support at each piece of gymnastics equipment.*
You have worked on traveling across, up and down, and under the equipment. Transfer out of each balance, travel to a new location on the equipment, and create the next balance—all without dismounting from the equipment. Remember to use smooth transfers out of balances and smooth transfers into balances.	*Have children rotate through the stations so that they work equally at each one.* *Review the importance of relationship of body parts (chapter 4), such as hands close together or apart. This relationship becomes increasingly important as students are balancing and traveling on different pieces of gymnastics equipment. Provide individual feedback as needed.*
Choose the place on the equipment for your first balance. Balance on your chosen bases of support. Travel to a new location on that equipment and balance on different bases of support. Repeat with travel to new location and balance on different bases of support. The series will be balance #1, travel; balance #2, travel; balance #3, using different bases of support for each balance and different ways to travel between each balance. Plan for a smooth transfer into a balance and a smooth transfer out of the balance.	*Emphasize stillness in balances and smooth transfers into and out of balances.*

FIGURE 7.3   Balances demonstrated on mat before equipment.

Balances on varying bases of support.

Photos courtesy of the authors.

LEVELS

Learning experiences	Teaching tips
Challenge yourself for balances and travel at different levels on the equipment, remembering that you can travel on top, under, and along the sides of the equipment; your balances can be at high, medium, and low levels. A change in levels may determine the weight transfer you choose into your next balance.	*Continued work and rotation at stations.* *Emphasize levels in relation to the student's position on the piece of equipment, not in relation to the floor. Children may need individual assistance as they explore this concept. It is quite different from levels when working on the mats.*
Challenge: Create a series of balances and travel at your favorite station: three balances, three levels, with travel between each. Show your series to a partner at that station; they will serve as the coach to give you pointers for better balances, weight transfers, or travel. When the series of balances, levels, and travel is your best, record it with stick figures and place it in your portfolio. Don't forget to serve as the coach for the partner who helped you.	*After students have completed a full rotation to all stations, they select a favorite station for the challenge.* *If you observe many students at one station and few or none at another station, call this to the attention of the class and remind them of the link between number of students at a station and practice time at that station.* *Distribute paper and pencils to children and give directions on recording work and placement of paper and pencils when moving to the next station. Remind students to put their name on their paper; otherwise, it is just a piece of paper.*
Challenge: Select one other station for a change in the configuration of the equipment. How does this change your choice of balances, levels, and your methods of travel? Complete your series of balances and travel at this station. Don't forget the stick figures.	

Folded mats as equipment option for balance.

SHAPES: 4 + 2

Learning experiences	Teaching tips
Your work today will focus on balances and body shapes. We call it the 4 + 2, the body shapes of wide, narrow, curled, and twisted plus symmetrical and nonsymmetrical. Explore balances in the body shapes of wide, narrow, curled, and twisted on the equipment. Remember that you may make these shapes with the total body or with body parts. You may stay in one location as you change to wide, narrow, curled, and twisted shapes. Or, you may travel between balances, changing your bases of support and shape for each balance. Record your balances at each station. If you traveled between your balances, be sure to record that also.	*Students will begin a new rotation of stations for the new learning experiences. They need paper and pencils for the drawings of shape balances. Remind children of the protocols for recording balances.* *As children work at different stations and create balances with transfers and travel at each station, the recording of those balances with paper and pencil will help them build their repertoire of balances on equipment.*
Explore balances with symmetrical and nonsymmetrical shapes on the equipment. Remember that these are the shapes with the total body appearing the same on both sides (symmetrical) or the body not being the same on both sides (nonsymmetrical).	*As you observe you may notice some children using the same series for each station; others are creating quickly with little thought to remembering the series. Encourage children to challenge themselves at each station for variety of balances, travel, and full use of all surfaces of each piece of gymnastics equipment.*
Explore different bases of support using the 4 + 2 body shapes.	*Remind children that the focus is on bases of support as well as body shapes for each of their balances.*
Record your combination body shape and bases of support balances on equipment for your portfolio. You now have several balances recorded on your personal worksheet. Your stick figures show shapes, bases of support, and levels as well as a series of balance, travel, balance. These drawings will be helpful in your later work on the gymnastics equipment as you select your best balances and your best station for sequences.	*Remind students to record their balances at each station as they are working rather than wait until the end of class to record all their work for the day.*

VARIETY AND QUALITY IN BALANCES AND TRANSITIONS

Learning experiences	Teaching tips
You have worked at various stations, but the focus has been the same at each one: balance, weight transfers, and travel. You created balances on different bases of support, at different levels, and with different body shapes. That's a large number of balances. You recorded those balances with stick figures. Take a few moments to look at the balances you drew on your paper. Ask yourself the following questions:	*Allow time for students to work at stations of their choice to improve their personal worksheet of balances for variety and quality.*
	Review the protocol for selecting a station, working safely, and changing to another station.
	Remind children of the procedure for using pencils and personal worksheets as they change stations.
• Did I use different bases of support? How many?	*As you observe the class working independently, provide feedback for the class and for individuals, focusing on quality of balances and transfers: stillness in balances, smooth transfers, flow of movement into and out of balances.*
• Were my balances different as I changed to a different station for my work?	
• Do I need more variety in my balances? If so, how can I create variety and quality in my work?	
• Is there a station or stations I need to return to for more work?	
Would you like to spend a few minutes at a station to improve your balances after reviewing your balances with the preceding questions?	
Return to that station to create some new balances or change some of your balances.	

GYMNASTICS EQUIPMENT MOUNTS AND DISMOUNTS

Children's work on educational gymnastics equipment begins with exploration of the various pieces of equipment with a focus on safety. They learn to get on the equipment, explore traveling on the equipment, and getting off with a return to the feet. This awareness of the challenges of the equipment, the comfort level for personal skills, and the overriding concern for safety and personal responsibility establishes the foundation for all work on gymnastics equipment.

As students progress in their work on gymnastics equipment, the challenges of mounts and dismounts arise as part of their sequences, thus the need for focused work on getting on and getting off each piece of equipment. These areas of skill development are exciting to children, especially the dismounts as they explore jumping from equipment, transferring weight to different body parts other than feet for getting off, and challenging themselves in the increased height for in-flight actions. The learning experiences that follow are designed to develop those skills for younger children with exploration and single balances, and for all children as they progress through the learning experiences in readiness for sequences on the equipment.

Exploration of Mounts Onto Equipment

Cognitive: Decision making includes how to mount considering body parts used, safety, and travel approach. Selection of mount may be based on height and configuration of the equipment.

Skills: Mount equipment safely in a variety of ways using climbing and jumping actions (both one-foot and two-foot takeoffs). Transfers from feet to body parts other than feet. Travel options for approach.

Criteria: Smooth and safe transfer onto equipment. Smooth travel movements in approach to equipment.

Safety: Skills for getting on matched to individual skill of student. Correct selection of mount. Spatial awareness of others when approaching equipment with traveling action.

Equipment and organization: Educational gymnastics equipment positioned with adequate spacing between and around all pieces of equipment, sufficient space for safe travel into mounts. Paper and pencils, protocol for recording work and storage of worksheets at the end of class.

MOUNTING FROM A STATIONARY POSITION

Learning experiences	Teaching tips
You have created several balances on different pieces of gymnastics equipment: bars, beams, platforms, ladders, bridges. You have traveled on top, under, around, and through the equipment; you have traveled on feet, on hands, and on numerous other body parts. You have created balances on different bases of support, at different levels, and with different body shapes. Aren't you glad you recorded your work with the pictographs using stick figures? The amount is almost overwhelming. Your work today adds another dimension to gymnastics on equipment—getting on the piece of equipment.	*With students in personal space, review safety rules in general and specific to individual equipment.* *Name each piece of equipment as you discuss the safety involved.* *See figure 7.4.*
At each of the stations, you will explore different ways for getting on the equipment and transferring into a balance: • Climb onto a lower rung of the ladder and balance on knees and hands. • Jump onto the bench using either a one- or two-foot takeoff (bench, bottom bleacher, folded mat), and balance on one foot with free body parts extended. • Standing at one end of the vaulting box or platform, place your hands on either side of the box and jump onto the box, landing on your knees and lower legs. You may balance on knees only; on knees and hands; on knees, hands, and head. • Using a two-foot takeoff, with hands on either side of the platform, jump into a balance on your upper thighs. Transfer from the balance onto the platform for another balance on different bases of support. • Standing under the curved bridge or horizontal ladder, jump to reach the ladder with both hands. Balance with legs in a wide shape. These are examples of climbing and jumping onto the equipment. You will discover many more as you explore the "getting on" part of working on gymnastics equipment. Some pieces of gymnastics equipment dictate whether you need to climb or jump onto the equipment; for others you have a choice.	*Divide students into equal groups for stations.* *Remind the class that all mounts onto the equipment are from a stationary position; they do not run to the equipment.*

Learning experiences	Teaching tips
Think ahead to what your first balance on the equipment will be. Design your "getting on" with that balance in mind. The match between getting on the equipment and the first balance creates a smooth transition—another form of weight transfer.	

 Explore your options at each station, remembering that safety is paramount in gymnastics.

Learning experiences	Teaching tips
Remember that a one-foot takeoff is a stepping action; feet touch the floor or surface alternately (climbing onto equipment; walking on beams, benches, bottom bleachers; feet-hands-feet travel actions). A two-foot takeoff is needed for jumping onto equipment and jumping upward to bases of support other than feet.	*Discuss with the class the difference between a one-foot takeoff and a two-foot takeoff and the use of each in gymnastics. This distinction will be important now and in their future work of mounts and dismounts.*

FIGURE 7.4 Sample mounting equipment.

MOUNTING WITH TRAVEL, CLIMBING, AND JUMPING ACTIONS

Learning experiences	Teaching tips
Take 8 to 10 giant steps away from the piece of equipment on which you are working. You are now going to travel from that spot to the equipment and then do the mount and balance you have practiced. Be creative; this one is fun. You can travel on your feet, on hands and feet, or on other body parts. You can turn and spin, leap, gallop, skip, or run. Practice several ways of approaching the equipment and then select the one you like best, the one that fits your transfer onto the equipment. This transfer is called the approach.	*Introduce the new learning experiences only after students have rotated to all the stations for the previous work. A new rotation begins with these experiences.* *Adding the creative approach and requiring only one or two balances support individual differences and success for the less skilled and for younger children.*
Approach the equipment with your favorite travel movement, transfer onto the equipment, and balance on your favorite bases of support.	*Emphasize the importance of a smooth transition into the balance after the mount onto the equipment.* *Remind students of three to five seconds of stillness for balances.*
You will create an approach, mount, and balance at each station as you work today. You may want to record the series on your personal worksheet because you will create one at each station. Remember that quality and variety are your goals for all gymnastics work.	

Exploration of Dismounts From Equipment

Cognitive: Dismounts from equipment include jumping and transfers from other body parts. Jumping off equipment is a combination of jumping high and forward (sufficient forward movement must be present to avoid contacting the equipment when descending from the jump).

Skills: Landing safely from all pieces of gymnastics equipment. Jumping with a two-foot takeoff for height.

Criteria: Safe landings, match between balance and dismount for smoothness. Safe landings for all dismounts. Landing on two feet shoulder-width apart with knees bent, alignment, and head erect.

Safety: Awareness of spatial needs of others. Adherence to all safety protocols.

Equipment and organization: Gymnastics equipment of differing heights and configurations. Appropriate equipment for jumping dismounts. Mats under the equipment and at the ends for dismounts. Equipment appropriate for the learning experience is listed in parentheses within the task. Self-responsibility and safety adherence are critical when children begin exploring dismounts from equipment. The organization of groups and equipment provides increased safety for this work.

 Dismounts from equipment should not be taught unless mats are in place surrounding, under, and leading to and from the equipment to ensure children's safety.

BALANCES AND TRANSFERS TO DISMOUNTS

Learning experiences	Teaching tips
The focus of your work today is getting off the equipment after you have completed your balances and transfers. This action is the dismount, leading to the end of your series on the equipment. The dismount is often determined by the height of the equipment, the configuration of the equipment, and the angle of the equipment on which you are working—vertical, slanted, or horizontal. As was true for getting on the piece of gymnastics equipment, the equipment sometimes determines the dismount; other times you have options.	*With students in personal space, not on equipment, review the protocols for safety with gymnastics equipment.* *For children inexperienced in working on gymnastics equipment and for younger children, you as the teacher need to determine the height that is safe for children to get off the equipment by jumping.* *Some children will also need guidance, or direct instruction, about the type of dismount action that is safe for the piece of equipment and for the individual.*
When you begin working at your station today, choose a favorite of your balances on that piece of equipment. This will be the ending balance before your dismount from the equipment. After three to five seconds of stillness for the balance, jump from that equipment to the floor, using a soft, safe landing (from bench, low beam, bottom bleacher, low steps, vaulting box, or platforms of appropriate height).	*Have students rotate to new stations for learning experiences.* *Remind students that the type of dismount they select will greatly affect what they choose for the balance.*
Balance at a low level, transfer your weight to balance on hands and knees, knees and feet, or on your stomach. Place your hands on the mat, tuck your chin, twist slightly, and transfer to the mat with a forward safety roll (bench, platforms of appropriate height). 🚧 **No forward rolls, no backward rolls—only safety shoulder rolls.**	*Observe closely as children are working; stop and reinforce safety rules at any time, such as using shoulder rolls only.*
Balance on one foot with free body parts extended. Transfer your weight momentarily to hands only on the equipment; then transfer to the floor, landing on both feet, with alignment and no loss of balance (bench, low beam).	*Some children are hesitant about taking weight on hands on equipment. A demonstration will be helpful to show how the transfer is made for the dismount. The transfer can be at low level with a small extension, thus easing concerns of those less skilled.*
Challenge: Either from a one-foot balance or from travel by walking, transfer weight to hands only (vaulting box, platforms). Transfer weight to the floor, landing on both feet, with alignment and no loss of balance.	*See figure 7.5.* *Emphasize with the class that the previous transfer to hands is also a correct response to the task.*
Hang from your hands under the equipment and drop to the mat, using a balanced, safe landing (horizontal ladder, curved bridge).	*Emphasize using safe landings, always.*

(continued)

Learning experiences	Teaching tips
Balance on your favorite body parts on the inside or outside of the bars. Climb to the lowest rung on the ladder, step to the mat, transition into a new balance on the mat, and then end with the "Ta-da" (vertical ladders, triangles).	*This action is now a gymnastics series ending with the "Ta-da."*
Explore dismounts from equipment in different configurations, from balances with different bases of support, and at different levels. Focus on safe landings and smooth transitions from balance to the ending "Ta-da."	*Emphasize smooth, flowing transitions from balance into dismount.*

FIGURE 7.5   Balance, weight on hands, dismount onto feet.

Jumping Off Equipment With a Two-Foot Takeoff

Cognitive: Jumping off equipment is a combination of jumping high and forward (sufficient forward movement to avoid contacting the equipment when descending from the jump). See figure 7.6.

Skills: Jumping and landing off equipment with a two-foot takeoff and two-foot landing. In-flight shapes and actions.

Criteria: Safe landings on two feet, shoulder-width apart with knees bent, alignment, and head erect. Quality in-flight actions.

Safety: Balanced landing on mats, making sure that area is clear of others before jumping.

Equipment and organization: Gymnastics platforms of appropriate height and structure for jumping off, such as bottom bleacher, low stages (4 feet [120 cm] high or less), vaulting boxes, aerobic steps, wooden boxes, folded mats, low sturdy tables. Mats surrounding equipment and extended at the ends for landing. The selection and organization of the gymnastics equipment is for these specific learning experiences; do not substitute inappropriate equipment.

 Do not use equipment unless sufficient mats are in place surrounding the equipment and extended for jumping and landing from the equipment.

FIGURE 7.6 Dismount with two-foot landing.

SAFE LANDINGS FROM NEW HEIGHTS

Learning experiences	Teaching tips
The gymnastics equipment has been rearranged today. Some pieces have been purposely removed from the work area for the task you will be practicing: jumping off the equipment and landing safely. There are slight differences in the height of the pieces of equipment, but all are a height I have determined will be safe for your jumping and landing. All dismounts will be with two-foot takeoffs, leading to experiences with in-flight actions and shapes.	*As children progress in skill development and in height, pieces of gymnastics equipment that are at a greater height may be included. But jumping should never occur from the rungs of ladders, vertical or horizontal, or from bridges.* *With students in personal space, not on equipment, review the safety rules for gymnastics. Allow time for questions and discussion.*
Let's review the criteria for safe landings. Tell your neighbor the important parts of a safe landing. If you heard, "Landing on two feet, feet shoulder-width apart, alignment of hips over feet and shoulders over hips, and head erect," you heard correctly. Then tell yourself, "No loss of balance."	⚠️ ***Children must follow the protocols for safe landings when jumping from equipment. Review, discuss the reasons for the rule, and never allow a student to infringe on those rules.***
Stand in a balanced position near the edge of the equipment on which you are working. Jump off the equipment, landing in a balanced positioned on the mat. After several jumps, ask the person who jumped before you to observe your takeoff and landing and give you a thumbs-up if correct: soft landing with knees bent, alignment of hips over ankles and shoulders over hips, and head erect.	*Divide the class into equal groups for work at stations.* *Continue practice with rotation of stations until everyone is demonstrating safe landings. If a child continues to have difficulty with the landing, provide individual feedback or assign them to the station with a lower height.*
Jumping from gymnastics equipment with a two-foot takeoff is a vertical jump with a slight forward action. You will need height for shapes in the air; you will need a forward jumping action to avoid crashing on the equipment as you descend from the jump. Practice your jumps, slightly increasing the height of the jump until you attain a 2- or 3-foot (60 or 90 cm) clearance from the equipment when you land on the mat.	*Students need a rotation to each station and a thumbs-up for safe landings before the next learning experience is introduced.*
When you can consistently jump (three times, thumbs-up from partner) from the equipment with correct landings and clearance of the equipment, increase the height of your jump for maximum in-flight time. If you touch the equipment or lose your balance on landing, revert to a lesser height and practice again.	*Emphasize self-responsibility as students increase the height of their jumps.*

JUMPING WITH IN-FLIGHT ACTIONS AND SHAPES

Learning experiences	Teaching tips

Jump off the equipment, creating a narrow shape while airborne, with arms stretched high above the head, legs stretched and close together. Remember the criteria for the landing: feet shoulder-width apart, knees bent to absorb landing, alignment, head erect. You may want to extend arms forward as you land for better balance. "Ta-da."
 	
  Remember that for all in-flight actions, you must be able to return to a safe two-foot landing.
	See figure 7.7.
	
	  When students are combining travel on equipment with jumping, shapes, and turns, safety dictates that students travel and dismount one at a time. The second person does not begin travel until the student in front has completed their safe landing.

Jump from the equipment, creating a wide shape while airborne with legs extended for the wide shape. Arms may still be extended upward for more height on the jump. Arms extended forward will provide better balance. Safe landings. "Ta-da." **Remember, be aware of space, height of your jump, and the time you have in the air. All are extremely important for a safe landing from these jumps.**	*Observation of concentrated time on task, avoidance of fatigue, and sufficient practice time at each station are important as skills advance. Don't rush students for completion of all stations in one class time. If the rotation is not complete, establish the protocol for the beginning of the next class.*
Challenge: Jump from the equipment, creating a round shape by curling the body at the height of the jump. Legs and arms pulled close to the body momentarily complete the curled or rounded shape. Recover quickly for a safe landing. You do not have to curl your entire body; stay within your comfort zone. Keep your head up, looking forward to help with a safe landing.	*Emphasize the quick recovery for a safe landing. Remind students to work within their comfort zone for this challenge.*
Jump from the equipment, creating a twisted shape by twisting the body while at the height of the jump. Untwist the body for a safe landing.	*Review twisting action from earlier work. Remind students of the importance of safe landing.*
Jump from the equipment, creating a symmetrical shape in the air, then a nonsymmetrical shape.	
Jump from the equipment, creating your favorite shape while airborne. Land safely, lower the body into a safety shoulder roll or a sideways roll, and end with a balance. "Ta-da."	*Remind students of the order of the components of the series: jump, airborne shape, safe landing, safety roll, balance, "Ta-da."*
Jump from the equipment with a quarter turn while airborne. Practice turning clockwise and counterclockwise. Safe, balanced landings are important with turns while airborne.	*Emphasize safe landings with airborne turns.*

(continued)

Learning experiences	Teaching tips
Jump from the equipment, using your favorite shape or turning action while airborne. Land safely, transfer your weight with a feet-hands-feet action, and create an ending balance.	*Remind students of the components and the order for the series.*
Travel across the beam or bench, stop and balance on two feet, dismount with a two-foot takeoff and a favorite shape or action while airborne, land safely, and finish with an ending shape.	*Emphasize quality of balance and actions, with flow of movements.*

FIGURE 7.7   Sample in-flight shapes off equipment.

SEQUENCES ON EQUIPMENT

The culmination of children's work on gymnastics equipment is the creation of sequences. The sequences may be as simple as getting on the equipment, creating one or two balances, transferring out of the balances, and dismounting from the equipment. Or the sequence may include an approach; a mount; balances; transfers of weight; levels; shapes; stretching, curling, and twisting actions; a dismount from the equipment; and an ending shape. Depending on the foundation of learning experiences for the children and the teacher's awareness of their skill development and readiness, decisions will be made regarding the complexity of the sequence. Inexperienced and younger children will be asked to create less complex sequences than experienced students who have a background of work in educational gymnastics on equipment. Either way, the teacher establishes the requirements for the sequence, encouraging the children to expand on those requirements for their unique sequences. Chapter 6 provides excellent guidelines for the teacher in the development of educational gymnastics sequences for both the experienced and the inexperienced learner.

Individual Sequences on Equipment Overview

The learning experiences that follow provide specific guidelines for sequences on equipment. The complexity of those sequences will be determined largely by children's previous skill development and cognitive understanding of the balance and weight transfer learning experiences and sequences on mats. Factors such as how many days per week students come to physical education and the time interval since students last worked on sequences on the floor will influence those decisions (chapter 3).

The sequences will be developed as they were in chapter 6, starting with the middle, adding the ending, and finally incorporating the beginning. This order helps with the connections and flow of sequences. Do not rush the process. Students need ample practice time to create and to perfect their sequence. The process likely will take more than one class period.

A template for gymnastics equipment sequences can be found at the end of this chapter in appendix B. Students will share their sequences with a friend at each stage of their development and with you, the teacher, when complete. The final sequence assignment, with positive comment by peers and by you, is then ready for the child's portfolio, perhaps to be shared as a summative assessment (chapter 8) with parents at an evaluation conference.

Individual Sequences in Action

Cognitive: An understanding of the requirements of the sequence.

Skills: Create and perform a sequence that meets the requirements set by the teacher.

Criteria: Provided in the requirements of the sequence. Balances held for three to five seconds. Smooth, flowing transitions. Variety and creativity. Safe landings.

Safety: Use equipment safely and correctly. Spatial awareness of others.

Equipment and organization: Age-appropriate educational gymnastics equipment with mats placed for safety, pencils, sequence templates. Equipment positioned with adequate spacing between, around, front, and back for mounts, dismounts, balances, and transfers on equipment. Sequence requirements listed on the whiteboard or screen, final assignment sheet for recording of sequences, protocol for recording sequences, storage of written work and pencils at end of class.

 Students should not use any piece of equipment for sequences unless sufficient mats are in place surrounding, under, and leading to and from the equipment to ensure children's safety.

CREATING AND PERFORMING INDIVIDUAL SEQUENCES

Learning experiences	Teaching tips
In your gymnastics work on equipment, you have balanced on different bases of support, in different shapes and at different levels. You have practiced transitions between balances and travel on, under, around, and through the equipment. You created unique ways for getting on and getting off the equipment (mounts and dismounts); you even developed the skills of shapes and actions while airborne after jumping off the equipment. And then, just for fun, you created an approach to the equipment that was unique and totally just you.	*Children seated in personal space, near the teacher, with personal worksheets from previous lessons.* *Children may need guidance in the selection of the best station for their work. A review of their personal worksheets may help in this decision.*
Now you know why you were asked to record all that work on your personal worksheet; you now have a wealth of gymnastics information. Today you will use all that learning to create a gymnastics sequence. Think of all the stations where you practiced balances, travel, and transfers. Where did you do your best work? That is probably the station where you will want to do your gymnastics sequence—the culmination of all your work.	*After the preceding discussion, students will be seated at the station of their choice for the development of their sequences.* *After students are seated at their favorite stations for the sequences, observe the number at each station. A large number of students at a station will result in less practice time for each child. Ask for volunteers to move to an empty station or to their second favorite station.* *Some students will wish to change to another station after they begin work on the sequence. Guideline: one change only.*
Let's review the basics of a gymnastics sequence. All sequences have a beginning, a middle, and an ending. Sequences on equipment also include an approach, a mount, and a dismount; thus, the requirements for your sequences on the equipment include the following: • A beginning shape • An approach—8 to 10 feet (2.4 to 3 m) from the equipment • Mount—getting on the equipment • Balances, weight transfers, and travel on the equipment • Dismount—getting off the equipment • Ending shape—"Ta-da" or other Your sequence will be composed of basic requirements that must be in all sequences. Although your sequence must include those items, you are not limited to them. You can add more balances, more travel, more of what makes your sequence unique to you. You can write or draw stick figures (pictographs) to show the details of your sequence.	*The sidebar Sample Individual Sequences provides three sample sequences, ranging from simple to complex.* *You as the teacher will make the decision about the particulars to be included in the sequence. The selection you make for your students will be based on previous learning experiences and skill progression of the class. Using a whiteboard, screen, or a separate handout, provide students the specifics for the sequence.* *Give each student a copy of the Final Sequence Assignment (appendix B) or create one that better fits the needs of your students. Review the recording of the components of the sequence, with stick figures and words.*

Learning experiences	Teaching tips
When you begin to design your sequence, begin with the middle—the balances, transfers, and travel you will do on the equipment. Will you add shapes, levels? Will you be satisfied with the requirements, or do you wish to add more? Work, think, and work some more. You will not be rushed. As you work on the middle of your sequence, the balances and actions on the equipment, remember the criteria: three to five seconds of stillness for balances, smooth transitions in and out of balances, variety, and quality.	*Describe the requirements of the sequence to the students. Provide directions for completing work on the equipment, recording that work, and working again.*
	Remind students that they can have help at any time, either from you or from a friend working at the same station.
	Students begin their independent work at their chosen station.
	As students are working at the stations creating their sequences, move to each station and observe for smooth transitions and still balances; provide refinement cues to the total class or to individuals. (Refer to chapter 6 for excellent refinement questions.) When they begin to practice the sequence in total, observe for continuity—the flow of the sequence from beginning to ending shape. This flow, with the individual's creativity and quality, is the sequence in its totality—the sum of all the parts. This can be the child's summative sequence for the portfolio.
You are now ready to add the ending to your sequence. Adding the ending when you have not done the beginning may seem a bit strange, but there is a reason. At the station where you have been working, do your last balance and then transition in readiness for the dismount. Remembering all the ways you explored dismounts from equipment, continue with your last balance on the equipment followed by a dismount from the equipment. Add the "Ta-da" for the ending of your sequence or a different ending shape. Now you are ready to practice all the work on the equipment, the dismount, and the ending shape.	*Review the criteria for safe landings if needed.*
	Some children will work quickly on their sequence; others will need guidance in getting started. Provide sufficient time for all children to practice, show to a friend, and practice again as they are completing the middle, ending, and beginning of their sequence.
	Remind them you are there to help.
And finally, add the beginning shape, approach, and getting on the equipment, the mount. The beginning shape is up to you, but it should signal you are ready to start your sequence. Practice the two or three favorite ways you created for approaching and getting on to the equipment to begin the balances, transfers, and travel.	*When they begin to practice the sequence in total, observe for continuity, the flow of the sequence from beginning to ending shape. This flow, with the individual's creativity and quality, is the sequence in its totality—the sum of all the parts. This can be the child's summative sequence for the portfolio.*
Challenge: Show your sequence to a partner at your station. The partner observing will be the coach and will provide suggestions for improvement or compliments for your decision making and skill. The coach will watch you one more time and write feedback on your sequence worksheet and sign their name. Change roles of coach and performer.	

Sample Individual Sequences

Sequence 1

- A beginning shape, an approach, and a mount onto the equipment.
- Three different balances on the equipment, each with a different base of support and with travel between the balances.
- Dismount off equipment, ending shape ("Ta-da" or other).

Sequence 2

- A beginning shape, an approach, and a mount onto the equipment.
- Three or four balances, each with a different base of support and a different level (or shape) for each balance and travel between the balances. If you choose a sequence of levels, you must demonstrate balances at each level. If you choose a sequence of shapes, you may choose to have balances that illustrate each of the four shapes or four balances with a combination of symmetrical and nonsymmetrical shapes.
- Dismount off equipment, ending shape ("Ta-da" or other).

Sequence 3

- A beginning shape, an approach, and a mount onto the equipment.
- At least five balances, with changes in levels, body shapes, different bases of support, and travel between the balances. Symmetrical and nonsymmetrical can also be an option.
- Dismount off equipment, ending shape ("Ta-da" or other).

Partner Sequences on Equipment Overview

Partner sequences are introduced as an option after students have created individual sequences on gymnastics equipment. Sequences with a partner on equipment are exciting with children discovering how to work with another person as they explore and create balances, weight transfer, and travel on selected pieces of educational gymnastics equipment. Partner sequences on equipment are recommended for the upper levels of elementary school physical education, for students with a background of learning experiences in educational gymnastics, and for students with a mature acceptance of self-responsibility and respect for others with whom they are working. Equipment that is suitable for partner sequences includes platforms of sufficient length for balances and travel (benches, beams) and climbing apparatus with connecting ladders or curved bridges. The following learning experiences for partner sequences on equipment are based on a functional understanding of the sequence work earlier in this chapter and the partner learning experiences found in chapter 6.

Partner Sequences in Action

Cognitive: An understanding of the requirements of the sequence. Communication and decision making with partner.

Skills: Create and perform a sequence that meets the requirements set by the teacher.

Criteria: Provided in the requirements of the sequence. Balances held for three to five seconds. Smooth, flowing transitions. Safe landings.

Safety: Use equipment safely and correctly. Spatial awareness of partner.

Equipment and organization: Age-appropriate educational gymnastics equipment with mats placed for safety, pencils, personal worksheet, final assignment template. Equipment positioned with sufficient space between, in front, and behind so that partners can move safely.

 Students should not use any piece of equipment for partner sequences unless it provides sufficient platform surface for balances, transfers, and travel by both partners; sufficient mats must be in place for children's safety.

EXPLORING PARTNER OPTIONS

Learning experiences	Teaching tips
Partner sequences on gymnastics equipment rely heavily on work you did earlier with partner balances on mats or the floor, as well as your recent work leading up to sequences on equipment. You will see on the whiteboard a listing of the terms and sketches from that partner work to illustrate each; these will assist you in remembering them. You learned earlier that all gymnastics sequences have a beginning shape, a middle section with balances and transfers, and an ending shape. Sequences on equipment have an approach, a mount, balances and transfers, a dismount, and an ending shape. The only difference for partner sequences is there are two of everything: two people with approaches, mounts, balances and transfers with possible travel, dismounts, and ending shapes. Working with a partner may be more difficult than working by yourself, but it is exciting!	*Students should be in listening position in personal space (not on equipment).* *Place the names and sketches of partner relationships, counterbalance, and other terms that the children studied in their earlier gymnastics work with partners on the whiteboard or on a poster in the work area.*
The choices of equipment for your partner balances are the balance beams (both low and high), the bench, and the climbing frames with a ladder or curved bridge connecting the two. The first discussion with your partner will be the selection of the equipment for your sequence; as before, you can change your mind one time before settling to work with your partner at that station.	*Partners at selected stations; teacher can select groups of three if necessary.*
Begin your work at the station by exploring balances that match those of your partner. Create balances on the equipment and balances with bases of support on the equipment and on the mat. • Create balances with matching levels, with matching shapes. • Create balances with contrasting levels—high and low, medium and low, high and medium. • Create balances that match symmetrical and nonsymmetrical. • Create balances that contrast symmetrical and nonsymmetrical.	*Emphasize the importance of cooperating with the partner for matching balances and travel. As in all educational gymnastics, recognizing the skill level of others is valuable.*

(continued)

Learning experiences	Teaching tips
Explore partner relationships, creating balances side by side with your partner, facing your partner, back-to-back with your partner.	*See figure 7.8.*
Explore balances and weight transfers with travel, meeting and parting with your partner.	
Explore counterbalance with your partner on the equipment, as a beginning balance, as an ending shape.	*You may need to review counterbalances from chapter 6.*

CREATING AND PERFORMING PARTNER SEQUENCES

Learning experiences	Teaching tips
You are now ready to put the parts together (beginning, middle, ending) to create a sequence of balances, transfers, and travel with your partner. The order of creating and working on these three parts differs for the partner sequence as compared with the individual sequence you did earlier. The work you just completed will help you make decisions for the middle. For now, begin with the beginning shape or the approach. The beginning shape can be on the floor followed by an approach, or it can be a beginning shape on the equipment. Either way, remember that the beginning says you are ready to start your sequence. One of the most difficult parts of the partner sequence is the timing of the actions; every move should match that of your partner. Not only will your balances match or contrast, the transfers and travel will also be in unison. The dismount and ending shape will be the last part of the sequence you create. The requirements of the sequence are the following:	*Partners at selected stations.*
	Remind partners they may ask another set of students to observe their sequence at any time to give pointers and to observe for quality and readiness for assessment. As with individual sequences, partners will come to you for observation when they are ready. Always add a positive comment after you observe their work. Peer assessments are an option while you observe.

- Beginning shape on equipment or beginning shape followed by an approach
- Four balances with weight transfers after each
- Changes in levels, shapes, bases of support, location on equipment
- Dismount
- Ending shape

Your choices for the sequence:

- Focus of sequence: matching and contrasting or meeting and parting
- Partner relationship: side by side, back to back, facing
- Counterbalance with partner as beginning shape, ending shape, or within the sequence

Learning experiences	Teaching tips
Don't forget to record in sketches and words all parts of your sequence on the assignment sheet.	*Partners join another set of partners using the same equipment. Share ideas for improvement and check for completion of written work.*

FIGURE 7.8 Sample partner balances on a bench.

Summary

Educational gymnastics on equipment takes all the skills of balance and weight transference and applies them to gymnastics equipment. With a focus on individual skill levels, a variety of height and configurations of equipment, all children, regardless of skill level or size, can be successful. Whether the child is experienced or inexperienced in the learning experiences has no effect on the criteria for quality. A focus on variety and creativity, with individual challenges, permits each child the freedom to explore and refine to their highest potential. Educational gymnastics equipment of ladders, bridges, beams, benches, and platforms of varying heights provides both the comfort and the challenge needed. Wonderful memories are made when a parent sees positive comments for quality, creativity, and skills about their child's work in gymnastics, either in a parent conference or in a report card packet sent home with the child.

Appendix A

TRADITIONAL GYMNASTICS BALANCE BEAM

The only piece of traditional gymnastics apparatus that fits within the elementary school educational gymnastics program is the balance beam. Traditional balance beams are 4 feet (120 cm) in height. Although many of the learning experiences on the low balance beam are applicable to the regulation beam, the added height presents challenges for mounts, balances, weight transfer, travel, and dismounts. The inexperienced student will be restricted by skill development and uncertainty, and the more experienced student will need individual responses to tasks and a high level of confidence for success. With the regulation beam set up with lower beams, benches, and platforms for travel and transfers, self-responsibility and challenges within individual skill levels will be extremely important.

 Remember that quality mats must be positioned on both sides and ends of the balance beam.

Balance under the beam.
Photo courtesy of the authors.

Older balance beams were wooden, presenting a pleasing visual to the observer and an extremely hazardous surface to the gymnast. **If your school has an older beam, it must be covered with suede or leather to meet the standards for safety.** Annual inspection of the balance beam will include the security of the bases to the beam and the security of the bases themselves, in addition to a tight fit of the covering on the beam. A balance beam that does not meet the basic requirements for safety must not be used in any gymnastics program.

Example Learning Experiences for the Regulation Balance Beam

- Approach the beam facing the length of the beam, the side. **Elementary school children should not be attempting to approach and mount the beam from either end.**
    - Children enjoy approaching the beam and then creating balances underneath the beam with travel to and from locations for balances.

- Prerequisites to mounting the beam can be as simple as balances underneath the beam and balances with combinations of bases of support on the beam and on the mats underneath.
  - Balance on the mat with shoulders and upper arms as the base of support. Extend legs and touch beam with feet.
  - Balance on one foot on the mat, extend arms forward to touch the beam, and extend free leg backward.
  - When children are ready (sufficient height and upper-body strength), a transfer of weight from the mat to the beam can be from feet to hands and upper thighs on the beam.
- A major challenge for elementary-age students is the transition from balancing underneath or on the side of the beam to a standing position on the beam. With exploration many children will discover this transition; others will need direct teaching for a successful transition to a standing position on the beam.
  - From the balance on upper thighs on the beam, swing one leg over the beam, balancing in a sitting position on the beam, with legs extended downward.
  - Transfer weight to knees and hands on the beam.
  - When ready, transfer to feet only on the beam.
- Travel on the balance beam is the same as travel on the lower height beams that children have already enjoyed. The increased height adds new challenges to existing skills.
  - Walk forward, backward, sideways on the beam.
  - Change directions with pivot turns.
  - Walk, alternating high level and low level with "dip steps."
- Balances can match the skill level of each student.
  - Balance on your base of spine, on your stomach, on knees and hands, on one knee and two hands.
  - Balance on combinations of body parts as bases of support.
  - Create balance at different levels, with different shapes.
- Dismounts from the beam can be either from the end of the beam or from a position along the length of the beam, from a balance or from travel.
  - For many children, this will be their first experiences of jumping and landing from this height; a two-foot, balanced landing is critical for safety.
  - **All dismounts from Olympic balance beams should be from feet to feet, using a two-foot takeoff at the side of the beam or a one-foot or two-foot takeoff at the end of the beam. All landings should be on two feet, landing on a quality mat. Dismounts with transfers from feet to hands to feet are reserved for after-school programs.**
- Individual and partner sequences are enjoyable and challenging options on the beam.

Group of three working on balance beam sequence.
Photos courtesy of the authors.

A balance beam of regulation height expands the possibilities of gymnastics for children. Presented with the tasks of mounts and dismounts, balances, weight transfers, and travel, the learning experiences are endless for the skilled student in educational gymnastics as well as the youngster beginning to make decisions about just getting on the beam. Within the environment of child-centered teaching and self-responsibility, the regulation balance beam is an excellent addition to the equipment of educational gymnastics for children.

From T.J. Hall and S.A. Holt/Hale, *Educational Gymnastics for Children* (Champaign, IL: Human Kinetics, 2024).

Appendix B

FINAL GYMNASTICS SEQUENCE ASSIGNMENT

Name:_____

Homeroom:_____ Partner:_____

Gymnastics Sequence (circle your choice):   Alone   Partner

Equipment Choice:_____

In the space below and on the back of this sheet, illustrate your sequence with a sketch of the equipment and stick figures for the balances. You may use words or drawings to describe the travel, levels, and shapes in your sequence. (Remember that if you do a partner sequence, you will have two figures for each balance and for each travel.)

The Approach: Beginning Shape, Travel

The Sequence in Figures and Words

The Dismount: Choice of Dismount From Equipment and Ending Shape

From T.J. Hall and S.A. Holt/Hale, *Educational Gymnastics for Children* (Champaign, IL: Human Kinetics, 2024).

PART III

Reflection and Assessment in Educational Gymnastics

Alignment of Goals, Standards, and Assessments in Educational Gymnastics

Chapters 1 through 7 have provided a framework for curriculum, an approach for child-centered teaching, and the learning experiences that lead to quality skill development in educational gymnastics. But these questions remain:

- What are your goals for the children you teach?
- How do you know your students have accomplished these goals?

This chapter addresses those two questions.

Physical Education Goals

Perhaps the larger question is this: What are your goals for the students you teach in your program of elementary physical education? What is the purpose of physical education in your school? In some schools, the physical education teacher is viewed as the person who provides planning time for classroom teachers or a break from their daily grind. For other schools, physical education is viewed as exercise for fitness and a time for children to get rid of excess energy so that they can listen better and do their work in the classroom. In these programs, success is measured by no one being sent to the clinic for injuries and no one being sent to the office for misbehavior. Success is students appearing to be "busy, happy, and good" in physical education.

The goal of physical education is to provide an individual with the skills, knowledge, and disposition to be physically active for a lifetime (SHAPE America 2014). Physical education is the foundation for physical activity. The skills and knowledge of physical education are not inherent within individuals; they do not automatically appear at a certain age in children. Those skills and knowledge come from the Movement Analysis Framework (see chapter 4). They are applied in games and sports, dance, and educational gymnastics and developed through learning experiences developmentally appropriate for the students being taught. Teaching for student learning comes from the elementary physical education teacher who has the content knowledge and a child-centered approach to teaching that focuses on individual children and their quest for quality movement.

National Standards

The question of curriculum remains. There is not a national curriculum for elementary physical education in the United States, but there are guidelines for curriculum content and expectations for student learning. Based on motor development and child development research, national standards for physical education first emerged in 1995. They defined what students should know and be able to do as a result of a quality physical education program. They also provided a framework to align instruction and assessment.

As the standards movement swept across the nation, all academic areas as well as related arts began to focus on the outcomes for students in that area of learning. States joined the standards movement by either adopting, adapting, or creating standards for education. Administrators welcomed the standards providing a measure of evaluation for teachers. Teachers welcomed the standards because they provided guidance for formulating goals and outcomes for student learning.

The standards have gone through revisions since 1995, but the focus on quality outcomes remains. Although states may differ slightly in their emphasis, and national standards have tweaked the language, all standards for physical education should share these components: skill development, knowledge, personal and social development (respect for self and others), value (enjoyment, challenge, self-expression, social interaction), and personal fitness. The educational gymnastics in chapters 1 through 7 is linked directly to these important outcomes.

Domains of Learning in Physical Education

The three domains of learning in physical education are the psychomotor, cognitive, and affective. All three domains are included in goal setting and are addressed in national and state standards. The psychomotor domain refers to motor skill and fitness development and is unique to physical education. Physical education, like the academics of the classroom, has a definite focus on the cognitive development of students. The affective domain refers to the development of personal and social skills and of value systems in children. Educational gymnastics brings opportunities for self-expression and joy to children as they challenge themselves without comparing themselves to others.

Educational gymnastics skills and movement concepts are found in the Movement Analysis Framework (chapter 4); the learning experiences in chapters 5 through 7 are based on those skills and movement concepts. The lifetime skill of balance (chapter 2) is the foundation of educational gymnastics. Balance and weight transfer are the psychomotor skills emphasized in the learning experiences in chapters 5 through 7. The focus is on quality individual skill development. The movement concepts are the basics of the cognitive domain of learning. Students must have a functional understanding of the Movement Analysis Framework to apply the concepts throughout the learning experiences in chapters 5 through 7. The learning experiences also highlight knowledge through the comprehension and application of balance concepts (chapter 5) and with numerous opportunities for higher-order thinking using exploration and problem solving (chapters 5-7). Children's cognitive process expands with self and peer analysis and evaluation, as described in chapters 6 and 7.

The child-centered approach to teaching, coupled with the content of educational gymnastics, highlights respect for self and others with a primary emphasis on self-responsibility. The goal is for students to take ownership in decision making and to move with a clear focus on body control and safety. Although all areas of formal schooling, academics, and related arts strive to develop the affective domain of student learning, physical education is rich in opportunities for positive development of the emotional and social growth and well-being of children. With a focus on meeting children where they are and providing the appropriate challenges for progress with no comparison with others, with the sharing of equipment and space, and with respect for others at all times, the affective development of children is greatly enhanced in child-centered programs of physical education. One of the joys of teaching educational gymnastics is seeing children attempt tasks they never dreamed possible and then having that moment of satisfaction when the task is completed and success is measured by a smile.

Lesson Objectives

The standards provide the expectations for students to attain at the end of their educational experiences, in this case, educational gymnastics. The daily planning begins with lesson objectives aligned with the standards. The teacher determines the objectives by considering teaching time, space, and equipment constraints (chapter 3). Other issues include the current skill, knowledge, and affective level of the students. Throughout chapters 4 through 7, we have avoided assigning grade levels to the learning experiences. Teachers can best determine their students' previous experiences with educational gymnastics and the prerequisite skills and movement concepts needed to progress the content.

In chapters 5 through 7, at the beginning of each series of learning experiences we include a focus title followed by points related to cognitive, skills, and criteria. The teacher determines how many of the learning experience series will be appropriate for the day. After making that determination, the teacher can select the skills and cognitive objectives using the information provided. The criteria are then used for measurements of success as well as the student and teacher focus for movement quality. Yes, the focus of child-centered teaching is on the individual student. Yes, children will have a range of skills and knowledge within each grade level and within each class. As with all teaching, the lesson objectives provide the expectations of the class. Knowledge of content and of the students informs the teacher how to navigate the variety of abilities within each class and remain child centered.

Reality of Grade-Level Benchmarks

Imagine a class of fourth-grade students in mathematics who do not have the prerequisites to the math concept you are introducing. Would you begin your teaching with the fourth-grade curriculum? Would your expectations for mastery be fourth-grade benchmarks? This is the teaching environment many teachers encounter when they first introduce educational gymnastics to their students. All students will be at the beginning level of balance as the foundation (chapter 5). As students progress in skill development and gain confidence in their skills, they will progress toward the established grade-level outcomes for both cognitive and physical skill development. Experiences in educational gymnastics within the program will lead to attainable grade-level outcomes.

This chapter began with two questions: What are your goals for the children you teach? How do you know your students have accomplished those goals? The first question has now been addressed. The standards and grade-level outcomes define the goals for educational gymnastics. The lesson objectives define the focus of a single day. The Movement Analysis Framework (chapter 4) defines the content; a child-centered approach (chapter 3) defines the teaching. The learning experiences of chapters 5 through 7 provide the tasks and challenges to meet those outcomes. Even equipped with the curriculum and the teaching style for success, however, the teacher cannot assume that these outcomes have been met. Assessment of student learning is necessary to answer the question of accomplishment of expected outcomes.

Assessment

Measurement of what students know, value, and can do is assessment in physical education. In the current climate of teacher accountability for student learning, teachers must provide evidence of meeting outcomes. Physical education is now sharing the same level of accountability as other subject areas. In a subject area often considered "not to count," physical education assessment can provide credibility with administrators and parents. Physical education teachers previously not being held accountable for student learning has resulted in loss of time allotted to physical education and in turn, loss of teachers.

Instructional Alignment

The connection of goals, outcomes, and lesson objectives to assessment and to instruction is called instructional alignment (figure 8.1). In other words, teachers should be assessing what they are teaching and teaching what they are assessing. As lesson objectives are written, the teacher determines what and how student learning will be assessed. This process ensures that the assessments are based on the objectives and that the teacher's goal is helping students achieve those objectives.

Formative and Summative Assessment

Assessment can be formative or summative. Formative assessment is assessment for learning, part of the daily teaching process with the idea that more opportunities for practice and improvement will follow. Summative assessment is assessment of learning, typically completed at the end of a series of lessons or a module or unit of specific content.

Formative Assessment

Assessment should be seen as the enhancement of learning, not just evidence of learning. In educational gymnastics formative assessment is an avenue to enhance learning, to inform students of progress, and to motivate students to continue to improve the quality of their work. Teachers are surprised to discover that they have always used some type of formative assessment. Teacher observation with specific feedback to students, opportunities for student self and peer checks, and teacher checking for understanding through

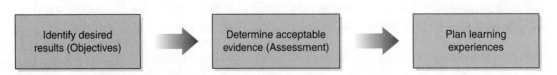

FIGURE 8.1   Instructional alignment.

Teacher provides feedback.

individual and class questioning are examples of formative assessment that many teachers have employed. Numerous examples of these are included and encouraged throughout the learning experiences.

Educational gymnastics as a child-centered approach places a focus on teacher observation of individual students. Throughout the learning experiences, we have provided reminders for the teacher to observe individuals. Based on the observation, the teacher prompts students who need help in the exploration or creating phase, encourages other students to challenge themselves, and provides individual specific feedback aligned with the criteria of the learning experience. In educational gymnastics, teacher feedback is designed to improve the variety and quality of student balances, weight transfers, and combinations of both.

Questioning within the lesson or at the end of class typically involves the teacher asking questions of the class followed by verbal student responses. Student cognitive engagement through questioning is beneficial and should be used often. For an idea of what all students know, written questioning and response can be in the form of an exit slip given at the end of class or an entrance slip given to students at the beginning of class. An entrance slip is a check for learning from a previous lesson, whereas an exit slip is checking for understanding the same day. They typically consist of one or two questions on a small piece of paper. The questions allow teachers to check for cognitive understanding (figure 8.2) or to evaluate the affective domain (figure 8.3).

Peer observation with feedback is another common and beneficial type of informal assessment. Both the observer and the active student gain from this experience. Peer evaluations can be a brief observation by one student followed by verbal feedback to a partner. They can also be a simple written checklist. Figure 8.4 is an example. Whether written or verbal, evaluations should focus on only one observation point at a time.

Formative assessments have another valuable purpose: The results inform the teacher of the quality of instruction. The assessment may prompt a decision to move the class forward immediately in the lesson or repeat, alter, or progress tasks for individuals. The results will be of value as a reflection for future teaching.

Summative Assessment

A summative assessment is designed to be documentation of learning that can be shared with parents or guardians, students, and when requested, administrators. Summative assessments require reliability; the assessment should be consistent in evaluation. Grading accurately and fairly is a necessity for summative assessment.

Name: _____ Homeroom: _____

Draw a stick figure doing one of your favorite balances that shows good extensions for counterbalance.

FIGURE 8.2 Cognitive entrance slip sample for grades 2 and 3.

From T.J. Hall and S.A. Holt/Hale, *Educational Gymnastics for Children* (Champaign, IL: Human Kinetics, 2024).

Name: _____ Partner: _____ Homeroom: _____

Circle the face that best describes how you feel about your experience working with a partner on counterbalance today.

	☺	😐	☹
Cooperation	☺	😐	☹
Communication	☺	😐	☹
Respect for each other's abilities	☺	😐	☹
Worked safely	☺	😐	☹

FIGURE 8.3 Affective exit slip sample for grades 3 through 5.

From T.J. Hall and S.A. Holt/Hale, *Educational Gymnastics for Children* (Champaign, IL: Human Kinetics, 2024).

Name: _____ Peer Coach:_____ Homeroom:

Coach: Watch your partner roll down the mat and back in a narrow body shape. Circle the response that best describes the roll for each direction.

Roll down: Roll is initiated by hip movement.	Yes	Somewhat	No
Roll back: Arms and head stay in a straight line with the body.	Yes	Somewhat	No

FIGURE 8.4 Peer evaluation sample for grades 3 through 5.

From T.J. Hall and S.A. Holt/Hale, *Educational Gymnastics for Children* (Champaign, IL: Human Kinetics, 2024).

Criteria: Balances held three to five seconds, muscular tension in base of support and free body parts, smooth transitions. Sequence is memorized and performed as shown on assignment. Goal aligned with criteria: three stars.

Level	Performed as written	Stillness	Muscular tension	Smooth transitions
★★★★	Sequence appears to be memorized, is performed as written, and can be duplicated on request.	All balances held for 5 seconds.	Muscular tension evident in base of support and free body parts. Extensions include hands and feet.	Well-executed transitional moves with no hesitation.
★★★	Sequence appears to be memorized and is performed as written.	All balances held for 3 seconds.	Muscular tension evident in base of support and free body parts.	Well-executed transitional moves with little hesitation.
★★	Part of sequence is not performed as written.	Some balances held for three seconds.	Muscular tension evident in base of support and free body parts.	Well-executed transitional moves with little hesitation.
★	Most of sequence is not performed as written.	One or no balances held for three seconds.	Little evidence of muscular tension.	Little evidence of smooth transitions.

FIGURE 8.5 Sample rubric for an individual sequence.

From T.J. Hall and S.A. Holt/Hale, *Educational Gymnastics for Children* (Champaign, IL: Human Kinetics, 2024).

Name: _____ Homeroom: _____

Observers: _____

Task: Perform a sequence with a partner that includes a beginning and an ending shape, three different balances, at least two different transitional moves, and one partner counterbalance. The counterbalance can be shown in the beginning or ending shape. Include somewhere in your sequence at least two of the following: locomotor travel, jump turn, jump with body shape in-flight, feet-hands-feet action.

Observer: Check yes or no

#	Sequence requirements	Yes	No
1	Beginning shape.		
2	Three different balances (base of support changes).		
3	Two or more transitional moves (each must be different).		
4	At least two of the following were included: locomotor travel, jump turn, jump with body shape in-flight, feet-hands-feet action.		
5	At least one partner counterbalance.		
6	An ending shape.		

I really liked the _____

_____

One suggestion for improvement is_____

_____

FIGURE 8.6 Sample checklist for a partner sequence.

From T.J. Hall and S.A. Holt/Hale, *Educational Gymnastics for Children* (Champaign, IL: Human Kinetics, 2024).

Summative assessments for the cognitive and affective domains are in the form of a brief written test that provides evidence of the knowledge and value gained from the educational gymnastics experiences. For the psychomotor domain, summative assessments called event tasks are typically used as a culminating experience when children are asked to apply what they have learned. At the conclusion of chapters 6 and 7, the individual and partner sequences can be used as event tasks. The sequences were designed to represent how students connected balance and weight transfers while demonstrating variety and quality—the focus of educational gymnastics. A rubric (figure 8.5) or a checklist (figure 8.6) of the criteria can be used to evaluate the sequences with reliability.

Throughout the learning experiences, we shared suggestions for students to use paper and pencils to draw and describe series of balances and weight transfers on the mats and on equipment and later for their creations of individual and partner sequences. Teachers are encouraged to use student portfolios to save individual work. Portfolio work encourages student responsibility and ownership of their work, and it says that the teacher cares about their work. The teacher or the student can decide what goes into the portfolio. Although much of the work in a child's portfolio includes formative assessments, the compilation of the work can be sent home to share with parents as a summary of the child's educational gymnastics experiences. Additionally, a portfolio with specific learning goals can serve as a summative assessment and scored with a rubric. The rubric would include clear criteria while encouraging student creativity. Portfolios can also be scanned and sent home electronically.

Summary

In this closing chapter we have posed and discussed, not answered, two questions: What are your goals for the children you teach? How do you know your students have accomplished those goals? The answer comes from the teacher, and we hope this chapter has helped in thinking about what learning should occur in the physical education program and how the teacher can be assured it has happened. We have provided three full chapters that include an abundance of learning experiences for educational gymnastics. When selecting the learning experiences for eager students of educational gymnastics, the physical education teacher must keep in mind instructional alignment, determine goals and objectives, and decide how to assess student learning.

Reflection Questions

1. Using the standards (state, national), make a draft of goals related to educational gymnastics. Begin with what students should know, value, and be able to do at the end of a K through 5 program.

2. Select one learning experience focus area and read the cognitive, skill, criteria, and all learning experiences aligned with that focus. Write two lesson objectives: a cognitive objective and a skill (psychomotor) objective.

3. Using the two lesson objectives from the previous question, create a cognitive and a skill written formative assessment. Use the sample assessment examples in this chapter to guide you. Remember that instructional alignment must be evident.

References

SHAPE American Society of Health and Physical Educators. 2014. *National Standards for K-12 Physical Education*. Author: Reston, VA.

EPILOGUE

We are delighted that you have chosen educational gymnastics for your physical education curriculum and a child-centered approach as your method of teaching children. We hope that the teaching of educational gymnastics with the focus on the individual child will bring you the same joy of teaching that we have experienced in our professional careers. Remember that the skills of educational gymnastics—balance and weight transfer—are not only the foundation of all areas of physical education but also the basis for a lifetime of mobility and wellness. From the toddler first gaining the ability to stand and walk to the older person maintaining that ability, balance and safe transfer of weight are critical components of life itself.

ABOUT THE AUTHORS

Tina J. Hall, PhD, is a retired professor in the department of health and human performance at Middle Tennessee State University. She taught elementary and middle school physical education for 18 years and has been in physical education teacher education since 2003. Dr. Hall has conducted numerous curriculum and content workshops and in-services for physical education teachers across the nation. She is a coauthor of *Schoolwide Physical Activity: A Comprehensive Guide to Designing and Conducting Programs* and *Teaching Children Gymnastics*. She joined the writing team for *Children Moving: A Reflective Approach to Teaching Physical Education* (in its 11th edition) in 2018. Dr. Hall is also an author of several articles in refereed publications.

Shirley Holt/Hale, PhD, is a retired physical educator from Linden Elementary School in Oak Ridge, Tennessee, where she taught physical education for 38 years. Dr. Holt/Hale is a former National Elementary Physical Education Teacher of the Year and has served as president of both the American Alliance for Health, Physical Education, Recreation and Dance (now SHAPE America) and the National Association for Sport and Physical Education. She is a coauthor of *Children Moving: A Reflective Approach to Teaching Physical Education* (in its 11th edition) and a contributing author for three other texts. She served as a member of the task force for the revision of the National Standards & Grade-Level Outcomes for K-12 Physical Education. Dr. Holt/Hale is a consultant in elementary physical education curriculum, assessment, and curriculum mapping throughout the United States.